'DEAD JAMMY!'

'DEAD JAMMY!'

The Life and Deaths of Scottish Undertaker Jammy Stewart

Allan Morrison

ILLUSTRATED BY

www.vitalspark.co.uk

The Vital Spark
is an imprint of
Neil Wilson Publishing Ltd
303 The Pentagon Centre
36 Washington Street
GLASGOW
G3 8AZ

Tel: 0141-221-1117
Fax: 0141-221-5363
E-mail: info@nwp.co.uk
http://www.nwp.co.uk

With grateful thanks to: Jim Crumlish, David and
Edith Easton, Jim and Irma Ireland, Andrew Pearson,
Claire Scott, Ron Williams and Archie Wilson.

Plus various 'men of the cloth' and undertakers,
who *definitely* wish to remain anonymous!

A catalogue record for this book is
available from the British Library.

ISBN 1-903238-75-7

Typeset in Bodoni
Designed by Mark Blackadder

Printed in Poland

Contents

Preface

Did you know that laughing 99 times each day gives your immune system and your heart and lungs the equivalent boost of 10 minutes of running? Not only is laughing good for maintaining your sanity, it lowers blood pressure and enhances circulation. Happier people tend to live longer, and away from the lugubrious clutches of the likes of 'Dead Jammy' Stewart, the undertaker.

If you intend to live forever – then, so far, so good. However there comes a time to consider your own mortality, and for most Scots it's about thirty seconds before they go to their celestial mansion or, more likely, wee but-and-ben in the sky. Eventually we are all chronologically challenged, past it, or have one foot in the grave, in which case people like Jammy will help you put the other one in. Dying is part of life; it happens to everybody. You could say it's exciting, for you don't know when it's going to happen. It's the final frontier, 'the great adventure', as Scots author J M Barrie once put it. Upbringing, religious belief and superstition are factors that contribute to a fear of the unknown. Death should not be mysterious or secretive. It is not selective because it stalks us all. Of course in modern parlance you're not really dead, you're just 'terminally inconvenienced'.

In this book I encapsulate the world of undertaking with all its quirkiness, humour and pathos, amply demonstrated by my hero, James Stewart, a Highlander, who ran an independent family funeral home in Glasgow for over 30 years. Nicknamed 'Dead Jammy', he was prone to

embarrassing mistakes, but always somehow seemed to manage to recover the situation, hence his nickname. Jammy's establishment specialised in funerals for fellow Gaels, the older generation, and Glasgow hard men.

An undertaker, posh name Funeral Director, should be able to solve the various problems posed at the time of bereavement, and maintain a dignified professionalism, irrespective of circumstances, towards those requiring his services. The Director is personally responsible for all details of a funeral, and must take control of events, giving guidance to mourners and staff alike. He or she must ensure that all vehicles are gleaming, and that floral tributes are properly loaded and disposed of in keeping with the families' wishes. Such an individual must be a top professional. And then there was Jammy!

These adventures of James Stewart, aka 'Jammy', also feature his unique communication style, a wicked, sometimes unfortunate mixture of Gaelic charm and mordant Glasgow patter, reducing many on occasion to paroxysms of mirth. His cheeky banter is rich in humour and warmth. When Jammy addressed the 'men of the cloth' he always called them, 'Yer Holy Reference'. And when the families of the deceased were of different faiths, Jammy would say, 'Ye should understaun, Yer Holy Reference, this wan's a 'mixed grill'. Women were always addressed as 'madom', men as 'kind sur'.

Of course drink and funerals in Scotland can be quite a deadly cocktail, sometimes resulting in mourners becoming involved in stushies and fisticuffs, which Jammy often had to deal with.

Fortunately for us all, Jammy has now joined his customers and truly is, 'Dead Jammy'. This means that your relatives will hopefully be spared traumas, embarrassments and 'cock-ups' at your funeral!

1

Scots and the 'Grim Reaper'

'Here's tae us; wha's like us?
Damn few, and they're aw deid.'

What do Robert Burns, James Watt, Sir Walter Scott, John Logie
Baird, Robert Louis Stevenson and up to a hundred million Scots
have in common?

They're aw deid!

And they were all dead lucky the funeral arrangements for
their rite of passage were not handled by 'Dead Jammy' Stewart.
It is said that funerals are important in coming to terms with
bereavement, unless of course the funeral director was Jammy, in
which case it could be a surreal experience.

Among all Scots, whether at home or abroad, there is an
almost spiritual affinity with the past. Even those families who
have made their homes in another land for generations are
compelled to remember their roots, clinging to their ancient
lineage with the skirl o' the pipes at their funeral, or their
remains returned to Scotland. We live as Scots and we wish to die
as Scots.

No one can see us before birth; none can see us after death.
There is certainly no rave from the grave. It is only in between
that we strut our stuff. The inevitability of death is all around us,
but we prefer the illusion of immortality because, of course, it
won't happen to us for years and years and years. And really
that's a healthy attitude, for we need to get on with life!

The trouble is Scots don't look after their bodies; they have
undertakers do that for them. They drink more than the English
because they buy rounds more often. We also tend to smoke more
than most. And then there's high cholesterol; many Scots are

unsure when this religious festival takes place!

So we laugh about our health, read our slimming magazines while eating fried Mars bars, toss down a few pints or six, cut our fags to 40 a day and say, 'Stuff mortality! Eternity can wait until ah finish ma bag of crisps. Who says ah'm diggin' ma ain grave wi' ma teeth? See health, it's strictly fur amateurs! Ah'm no' goin' oot joggin' wi' aw they 'coffin-dodgers'!'

Some folks say that death is nature's way of saying to wee Scottish widowers, 'Right, pal. Yer wife's waiting fur ye on the other side, and she's going tae give ye hell fur gettin' lumbered WI' that Jezebel in the next close after she went.' Or, if it's the other way round, the wee Scottish widow will be told, 'Yer man's waiting on the other side fur ye.' 'Is that so?' she'll reply. 'Well, ah bet ye he husnae even started makin' the tea yet.' Or perhaps it's like the Glaswegian who, when he saw the grim reaper, asked, 'Is that a sickle in yer haun or are ye jist goin' tae cut yersell a slice o' breed?'

Of course death is not quite the taboo subject it used to be. Scots now make varied and innovative arrangements for their own and relatives' funerals. The old, austere orthodoxies are not always used, and many funerals are arranged by folks before they go to include colourful and sometimes eccentric proceedings. Many eulogies now reflect the joys and fond remembrances of the deceased's life.

Anyway, people should take their leave of Scotland, and this life, as they wish.

Hindus go out in a blaze of glory. Salvationists are 'Promoted to Glory'. Moslems glorify in being buried facing Mecca. Some Scots might glorify in facing a distillery.

Many Scots have had most interesting funerals. There is the true story of Maggie Dickson, a fishwife, who was hanged in Edinburgh's Grassmarket in 1728. As her coffin was being taken for burial in Musselburgh noises were heard from within. Revived by a stiff dram she was allowed to go free, subsequently giving birth to a number of children and ultimately dying of old age.

Tobias Smollett (1721-71), in his *Humphry Clinker*, relays the goings-on at a Highland funeral. 'Yesterday we were invited to the funeral of an old lady, the grandmother of a gentleman in this neighbourhood, and found ourselves in the midst of fifty people, who were regaled with a sumptuous feast, accompanied with the music of a dozen pipers. In short, this meeting had all the air of a grand festival; and the guests did such an honour to the entertainment, that many of them could not stand when they were reminded of the business on which we had met. On arrival at the place of interment we found we had committed a slight oversight in leaving the corpse behind; so we were obliged to wheel about and met the old gentlewoman half-way, carried upon poles by the nearest relatives of her family. After the ceremony we returned to the castle, resumed the bottle, and by midnight there was not a sober person in the family, the females excepted. The squire afterwards seemed to think it a disappointment to his family, that not above a hundred gallons of whisky had been drunk upon such a solemn occasion'.

There are lots of interesting cemeteries in Scotland, many containing famous people. Glasgow has its Necropolis, a vast burial ground with grand gravestones and intricate weeping statues, where over fifty thousand of the City's famous and infamous sons and daughters rest their weary bones. There is a wonderful statue to William Miller (1810-72), the creator of Wee Willie Winkie, neither of whom now runs through the toon. The Necropolis was established next to the cathedral in 1832, and is based on the Pere-Lachaise cemetery in Paris, where amongst others, Oscar Wilde, Molière, Sarah Bernhardt and Jim Morrison of *The Doors* lie within a tombstone's throw of each other.

In Edinburgh, the Canongate cemetery, to the left of the

Royal Mile as you journey down to see the Scottish Parliament Building, contains the remains of many Scots of distinction. They include Adam Smith (1723-90), author of *The Wealth of Nations*, and David Rizzio, (1533-66) the favourite of Mary Queen of Scots, murdered in front of the Queen by husband Darnley and his henchmen. Nearby lie the earthly remains of William McGonagall (1825-1902), famed for, amongst many, his wonderfully appalling commemoration in verse of the Tay Bridge Disaster. Greyfriars, not too far away, owes its world-wide fame to a wee dog, Bobby, whilst St. Cuthbert's on Princes Street, hosts John Napier (1550-1617), the inventor of logarithms.

Further afield, Barra in the Western Isles, boasts the last resting place of *Whisky Galore* creator, Sir Compton Mackenzie (1883-1972), at St. Barr, Eoligarry.

Kilmuir, in Skye, has Flora MacDonald (1722-90), wrapped in a sheet slept in by Bonnie Prince Charlie. Dingwall cemetery has novelist Neil Gunn (1891-1973).

Iona has, amongst others, John Smith (1938-94), the Labour Party Leader. The churchyard at Spynie, Lossiemouth contains James Ramsay MacDonald (1866-1937), the first Labour Prime Minister.

The final resting place of Kings Malcolm the Fourth (1142-65) and Alexander the Second (1198-1249) is Dunfermline Abbey. Also there is Robert the Bruce (1274-1329), although his heart is interred at Melrose Abbey.

Scotland's National Bard, Robert Burns (1759-96) slumbers in St. Michael's Churchyard, in Dumfries, whilst his beloved 'Highland Mary' (1763-86), lies in Greenock Cemetery.

In the New Church cemetery at Kirriemuir is J M Barrie (1860-1937), who unlike his creation, Peter Pan, grew old and died.

At Gask, near Perth, lies Carolina Oliphant, (1766-1845), the songwriter responsible for *The Hundred Pipers, Bonnie Charlie's Noo Awa'* and *Will Ye No' Come Back Again?'*.

Yes, Scottish cemeteries provide wonderful places of quiet contemplation of our famous past and its peoples.

Until recently many Scottish obsequies consisted of various key rituals. When someone passed on, there was a morbid sense of loss felt by the immediate community. The blinds or curtains of the deceased's home would be closed until after the funeral. Mirrors would be covered, radios and televisions off. Neighbours would also show respect by pulling their blinds half-way down. In many tenement communities a woman naturally assumed the task of washing the body before laying it out. This was based on the premise that women are always present at birth and therefore should be there at the end of life. The undertaker would take the deceased away to prepare the body for burial, before returning it to the home. A suitable room, probably a bedroom or 'the best room', would be selected for the 'wake'. Relatives, friends and neighbours would come and pay their last respects, sometimes around the clock. They would bring with them food and drink of all sorts. This would provide constant company for the family in mourning. There would be much nervous chatter and recollection of anecdotes about the deceased, reminiscing being the order of the day. Some of these might be quite humorous. With the intake of alcohol the company at a wake could grow merry. On the other hand, old family disputes might once again come to the fore.

At Catholic wakes, the rosary would be said. In a Scottish community, neighbours took great pride in assisting each other at such difficult times, regardless of religious beliefs.

Before cremation was as popular or as accepted as it is today, it was not uncommon for families to buy a lair in the local cemetery. Some still do. Nobody wished to be buried in a cheap coffin in paupers' ground. This would be the final insult to them and their families.

On the day of the funeral, the priest or minister might come to the house to hold a short service before proceeding to the church for the full service or Requiem Mass. As a funeral cortege moved towards the cemetery or crematorium, passers-by would stop to show respect, men removing their hats and uniformed individuals would salute. At burials it was more traditional for the men to go to the graveside while the womenfolk stayed behind, perhaps preparing food for the returning mourners at the funeral tea. Usually it was drams for the men and sherry for the womenfolk, with plenty of tea and sandwiches.

But, dear reader, don't you worry. You've a long time yet and much damage to do afore ye go. So, grow old disgracefully. Don't just degenerate into old age. Have a bit of decadence. If you must suffer from some ailment, make it longevity. Enjoy the richness of a life that takes you along many paths, with laughter enhancing the way.

Like every culture, we joke about death and thumb our nose defiantly tae the grinning Reaper. After all, you came into this world after a good slap, then you had a bawl. So, before the ball is over, slap yer sides and have a good laugh with 'Dead Jammy'!

2

Introducing 'Dead Jammy'

Jammy was a fascinating sight as he strode purposefully in front of his hearse ... though sometimes, when it broke down, he was behind it ... pushing. It was well known in the district that if Jammy's hearse had a problem on the day of a funeral, then you got a discount.

Jammy had a lilting Highland tone, all underpinned by a confident style wrapped up in his trademark morning coat, hat, black tie, starched collar and dazzlingly white shirt, set off with gold cufflinks, dark blue waistcoat, complete with gold chain and Hunter pocket watch. His shoes were well polished, and a black handkerchief was stuffed with apparently careless arrogance into his breast pocket.

Jammy's face was round, almost boyish. The eyes would glitter with imminent mischief or shine innocently, especially when about to deny, with his usual aplomb, some obvious guilt. Jammy was a well-known, colourful character, someone who could quickly recover with great alacrity when things were going astray to become a maestro

completely in charge of all aspects of *his* show. A funeral director with a sense of subversive wit; a splendid tease. Someone who by turns was wickedly witty and wise. The man who unconsciously put the fun into funerals.

His old hearse, (nicknamed Lazarus, as it had to be continually brought back to life) plus two second-hand Humber Hawk limos, comprised the parlour's fleet. This usually made it a challenge for Jammy and his team of undertakers to get the coffin and mourners to the cemetery or crematorium on time.

Folks could be lying nice and comfy in their coffin in Jammy's parlour, trying to get some well-deserved eternal rest, when all around might be mayhem, caused by another wee mix-up by Jammy. Yet Jammy was also kind and thoughtful, respectful and understanding, sometimes adopting an attitude of avuncular indulgence when a poor family had difficulty paying for his services.

Most mornings he would stand, smoking a cigar, outside his establishment which was set in the ground floor of a decaying Glasgow tenement, beneath a sign which proudly read, 'Stewart Undertakers, Your Independent Privately Owned Funeral Directors. Chapel of Rest and Room of Repose available.' A smaller, more discreet sign stated, 'Try our Pay-Now, Go-Later Plan'.

Various undertakers in Scotland were given slogans by the local community. 'Go to Harkness, he'll bury your carcass.' 'Go to the Co-op, they'd bury a dope.' 'Go to Jammy, he'd start a rammy!' Now it must be said that Jammy wouldn't intentionally start a rammy, but occasionally when something went wrong, the relatives did get somewhat restless.

For all his mishaps, he had an old-fashioned view of the funeral business. 'Och, to be sure, ah'd bury onybuddy, indeedy ah would,' he once said, 'as long as they're deid. Mind you,' he added. 'there are some folks who urnae deid that ah'd still like tae bury!'

3

The Players in 'Dead Jammy'

Miss Teenan, the parlour's telephonist and receptionist. Better known as 'GFT', which she foolishly thinks means, 'Glasgow's Favourite Telephonist', when in actual fact it is short for 'Greetin' Faced Teenie'! A girnin', greetin', soor-ploomed, holy terror.

Harold Hudson, known to one and all as 'Happy Harry', a cheeky soul with bushy, brown hair rising in all directions. A face containing gentle, bright eyes, crows feet at the corners, indicating his propensity for laughter, even in the serious world of undertaking.

William McSquachles, referred to as 'Laughing-Boy'. Tall and grotesquely thin, with sharply cut features, particularly the beak-like nose. Always seemed to wear the same black, long, loose overcoat which hung from bony shoulders down to his ankles. This hid an ill-fitting dark suit, glazed through many years of continuous wear. A cigarette, with gravity-defying ash, always seemed to hang from the corner

of his mouth. He had never been known to smile, but as he had been with Jammy for years perhaps that was the reason.

Robert Ian Phillips, nicknamed 'RIP Van Winkle' due to his initials, having a passion for bowls, and a habit of dropping off for a snooze at a moment's notice. Always excused himself by saying he was practising for the 'Great Sleep'.

Flora MacDonald, Jammy's long-suffering girlfriend from the Islands. Would love to take him back over the sea to Skye, permanently. The owner of a florist shop in Glasgow much used by Jammy and his clients.

'Crazy Horse MacGonigal', the alleged ghost at the crematorium of the son of a North American squaw who had married a man from Maryhill! The result of some long forgotten,

alleged sighting by a lady
attending a funeral who had
over-imbibed prior to the funeral
tea.

'Tottie', the barman in
Jammy's local, the *Pigs and
Whistles*. Not always the sharpest
malt in the bar, an apparent
combination of Neanderthal man
and Glasgow numptie. Forever
asking questions about the
funeral trade.

Lazarus, also known as 'Fawnty', as in fawnty bits, the
parlour's ancient hearse. Prone to starting problems, especially
at the most inopportune times, Lazarus also gave forth a peculiar
wheezing noise when speeding along at more than ten miles an
hour. Once, on a somewhat wet and muddy journey through
Carmunnock cemetery, Lazarus returned to the parlour with an
inscription finger-written on the back, 'Rust in peace!' At least
old Lazarus had a heated rear window. This came in handy
during the winter, on the occasions when Jammy and his men
were pushing!

And then there is the Funeral director, the man himsel',
James Stewart ... 'DEAD JAMMY!'

+   +   +

Dead Funnies

The service was in the front room of a flat in a Glasgow high-rise
tower block. The coffin was in the nearby bedroom. 'Listen, yer
Holy Reference,' said Jammy to the minister. 'Could ye tak yer
time wi' the service as it's an awfu' wee lobby, and we'll huv a job
getting the coffin oot the door.'

   The minister duly extended the service as much as possible,
but was conscious of the time booked at the crematorium. At the
conclusion of the final prayer, the minister slipped out of the
room quickly to see how things were progressing, only to find
there was a problem. The key to unlock one of the panels in the
service lift was missing. 'We're going tae lose oor time at the
crematorium,' mumbled the minister.

'Dinny you fash yersel', yer Holy Reference,' said Jammy. 'We'll chest pit the coffin own its end and take it doon in the normal lift. Ah always make sure the feet are at the bottom.' The coffin was duly lifted upright into the small lift, Jammy and Happy Harry standing either side of it. Jammy pressed the lift button for the ground floor, and off it went.

At the third floor the lift suddenly stopped, and the doors opened. A wee woman in curlers and headscarf squeezed in. Taking a long draw at her cigarette and one look at the coffin, she observed, 'Ah see this lift's dead busy the day, eh? Standin' room only!'

+   +   +

The middle-aged man had come in to see Jammy a few days earlier. He had been making arrangements for his own pre-paid funeral, and had enquired as to the price of coffins. Now he had reappeared, somewhat red-faced, indeed indignant.

'How come, Mister Stewart,' he blustered, 'that you quoted me £200 for a coffin, and MacFarlane the Undertakers jist want £150?'

'Listen, man,' said Jammy, 'ah can explain efferything, indeedy ah can. Yer backside would go through their coffin in a fortnight. Mine wull last ye a lifetime.'

+   +   +

'Huv ye ever had ony bother gettin' wan o' yer 'customers' intae their coffin?' asked Miss Teenan one day.

'Chust the wance, GFT,' replied Jammy, a smile starting out on his face. 'By chove ah remember it well. It wis a wee bachle o' a wumman who died awfu' sudden like, in the middle o' the Hokey-Cokey at the Salvation Army's Christmas party. When we goat her back tae the parlour ah pit her left leg in ... then it aw started tae get a wee bit difficult.'

+   +   +

One day a man phoned Jammy, sobbing, 'Ma wife is deid. Can ye come an' dae the necessary?'

'But, chust a minute,' observed Jammy, 'did ah no' bury yer wife aboot eight years ago?'

'Yer right, Mister Stewart. Man, ye've goat a grand memory. But ah goat merrit again.'

'Och, ah see,' Jammy replied thoughtfully. 'Ma congratulations tae ye.'

22

+   +   +

Jammy was invited to the wake of an old drinking partner, Hector, originally from Ullapool.

The wake was being held in the 'best-room' of a small terraced house in Dennistoun. When Jammy arrived the room was crowded with folks, all standing around downing the cratur, many of them looking somewhat the worse-for-wear.

Hector's coffin lay on the table, in the centre of the room. Suddenly, it was announced that the foodstuffs would be appearing. The immediate question was where would the dishes go since the sideboard was already groaning with bottles. In a flash Jammy had the answer. 'Give me three chairs fur the coffin,' he instructed. 'Hip, hip hooray! Hip, hip hooray! Hip, hip hooray!' came the response.

+   +   +

'Listen you tae me, Happy Harry,' said Jammy one day. 'Ah've a wee job fur you, indeedy ah have. Aw they big undertaking firms have noo goat personalised number plates on their hearses. We've goat tae get ourselves up tae date. Could ye use a bitty o' initiative an' see whit ye can do fur Stewart Undertakers?'

A few weeks later Jammy ran into the parlour. 'Where's that Glesca clown, Happy Harry? Come here, you! Did ah no' tell ye tae get a nice new number plate fur Lazarus.'

'Aye, ah thought ah did a very good job, Jammy,' replied Happy. 'Ah used ma initiative like ye said. Everybuddy in Glesca wull see it. Probably get us mair business.'

'Probably pit us oot o' business, ye mean,' replied Jammy. 'Naebuddy wull be pleased when they see us driving by wi a coffin in the back, an' a number plate that reads, 'U2 1 DAY''.

✚   ✚   ✚

'Hey Jammy, huv you selected the music fur yer ain funeral when yer time comes?' asked Rip Van Winkle.

'Och, aye, indeedy,' replied a thoughtful Jammy. 'Goin' intae the crematorium ah want, '*So long, it's been good tae know you*'. At the end o' the service ah wid like tae frighten the life oot the competition wi', '*Ah'm no' awa tae bide awa*'!'

It's what he would have wanted!

A fussy wee man was in the parlour, making enquiries about pre-paid funerals. He also was also interested in determining the reputation of Stewarts the Undertakers. 'And just how many funerals have you held for dead people?' he asked Jammy.

'Aw ma funerals have been held fur dead people,' came the reply.

+   +   +

Jammy was sitting in the living room of the widow's flat, going over the details of the forthcoming funeral of her husband.

'Now, have you got ony questions for me, madom?'

'Aye. When does the best man give his speech?'

+   +   +

The bar was quiet, and Tottie was on his favourite subject, asking Jammy questions about the undertaking business.

'Ur cemeteries still popular,' he asked, 'noo that a lot of folks get cremated?'

'Och, indeedy aye,' replied Jammy. 'Why dae ye think they have tae have walls roon them?'

'Ah don't know,' mused the puzzled Tottie. 'Is there a reason?'

'Och, indeedy,' said Jammy. 'sure everybody is dying tae get in!'

+   +   +

The priest was asked to fill in at the last minute. It was not until he was accompanying the coffin down the church aisle for the funeral Mass that he realized he had forgotten to ask the gender of the deceased. As he approached the front he saw the familiar figure of Jammy Stewart. Reassured, he nodded towards the coffin and whispered, 'Brother or sister?'

'Cousin, yer Holy Reference,' replied Jammy.

+   +   +

'Listen you,' said the henpecked husband. 'ah've decided tae finally stick up fur masel'. There are going tae be changes roon here. First of all ah want mince and potatoes fur ma tea the night. Then ah'm going oot wi ma pals tae the pub. And ah bet you don't know who is going tae lay oot ma suit and polish ma good shoes fur me?'

His wife gave him a long, piercing look. 'Oh, ah know alright,' she said with venom. 'It'll be Jammy Stewart the undertaker!'

+   +   +

'Excuse me, Yer Holy Reference,' said Jammy to the Minister on the way back from the cemetery. 'At the graveside there, did ah hear ye correctly? Ah thought ye said, 'Ashes tae ashes, rust tae rust. Did ye no' mean dust tae dust?'

'Oh, no, Mister Stewart, you heard correctly,' replied the minister. 'Actually it was really a bit naughty of me, but I just couldn't resist it. You see, every time I visited him in hospital he was drinking Irn-Bru!'

+   +   +

The widow was in Jammy's office going over the arrangements for her husband's funeral. She had brought her daughter with her. The daughter was very upset, whereas the widow seemed totally unperturbed.

'Ma faither wis one in a million, Mister Stewart,' sobbed the daughter.

'Mair like won in a raffle!' corrected the mother. 'An' he wis the booby prize!'

+   +   +

'Ah see in the paper you've got a few funerals on tomorrow, Jammy. Who's deid?' asked Tottie.

'Och, that wid be the wans in the coffins.'

+   +   +

'Aye, an' another thing,' said the widow. 'Ah want his old pipe pit in the coffin wi him.'

'Och, right, madom. Noo, wid there be ony particular reason for that?' asked Jammy.

'Aye, Mister Stewart,' replied the lady. 'Ah wis always telling him the smell aff that pipe wis terrible, and tae get it tae hell oot the hoose. An' noo he's goin' there, he may as well take it wi' him!'

✛   ✛   ✛

The son came into the parlour to collect his father's ashes. The urn was duly handed over by Jammy's receptionist, GFT.

'Ah don't like tae be seen carrying this alang the street,' commented the man. 'Have ye no' goat any containers or plastic bags?'

'Jist a minute,' replied GFT, somewhat irritably. 'Ah've goat a carrier bag ah got in the bakers' this morning.' So saying, she put the urn in the bag and gave it to the customer.

'Hey,' protested the man. 'ah cannae pit ma faither's ashes in a bag that says 'Oven Fresh' oan the side!'

✛   ✛   ✛

Jammy was busy going over various details with the widow.

'Noo,' said the wee woman, 'ah wid like a verse inserted in the Notice of Death ye pit in the newspaper. Ma grandson made it up.'

Jammy looked at the piece of paper and his face didn't change as he said,' Och, very nice. Ah'll make sure it gets pit in.' It said, 'Nothing more can ever please us, Noo Wee Smelly's gone to Jesus.'

+   +   +

'He wis a fitness fanatic,' observed the widow, looking down at her dead husband. 'Took it tae extremes he did. Last year he gave up drinking, then he gave up the ciggies, followed by things like burgers and black puddin' suppers. Then, and ah shouldnae really tell ye this, he gave up sex.'

'So, whit killed him, madom?' asked Jammy.

'If ye ask me, bloomin' boredom!

+   +   +

'Is it true whit they say aboot there being a ghost at the crematorium?' Tottie the barman asked Jammy.

'Och, indeedy, it's true. Crazy Horse MacGonigal himsel'. In fact, Stewarts the Undertakers did his funeral.'

'And huv ye ever seen this ghost?' asked Tottie, eyes and mouth wide open.

'That ah huv,' replied Jammy, a mischievous grin crossing his face. 'Chust the wance, mind ye. It wis wan day the crematorium organist wis playing an awfa' haunting melody!'

+   +   +

It was the end of the day, and Laughing-Boy was describing an incident that had happened. 'Efter the first funeral this morning, wan o' the mourners fell doon the steps ootside the crematorium.'

'Och, ah'm no' surprised,' observed Jammy. 'Sure ah've always said that crematorium's a death trap!'

+   +   +

4
'Dead Jammy' and the Mafia

An unrelenting sun shone down on Glasgow. Eventually it was to prove to be the city's hottest day of the year. Café owners and purveyors of ice-cream throughout the city rubbed their hands with glee as hot, sticky citizens sought out Irn-Bru, Tizer, Coke and every kind of cooling ice cream.

Zarotti's café had a seemingly never-ending queue of customers; passers-by, women with prams and workmen. Then, when the schools came out later in the afternoon, it became pandemonium. The ice-cream machine hummed desperately as Toni and his wife Maria tried to keep up with the unprecedented demand. 'Whatta wonderfulla day furra business,' Maria observed to her husband.

Unfortunately, these proved to be the last words she ever said. Her heart gave out right in the middle of scooping out a double-nougat. She was dead before she hit the floor, leaving poor Toni devastated.

At the same time, in a residential home just a few miles from Zarotti's café, a highly competitive game of dominoes was in progress. Because of the heat it was being played on a table in the garden, in the shade of a large oak.

Harry Dingwall, formerly Sergeant Harry Dingwall, faced his opponents across the table, the shadows of the overhanging oak branches playing on his face. Harry was a former Glasgow and District Police Champion, a demon with the dominoes, and he was to be found every afternoon, and the occasional evening, taking on all-comers.

Maybe it was the heat. Maybe it was the tension of sitting with a double-six and nowhere to put it, Harry didn't know. But he felt himself get over-excited. With two chaps under his belt, he tugged his beard nervously waiting for that elusive six to play out and hopefully win before the tea bell.

It was only when one of the other players snapped, 'Right, Harry, hurry up and play. It's your turn. Are ye still chapping?' that it dawned on everyone that Harry had chapped for the last time ever. Someone shouted, 'Give him air, he'll be alright in a minute,' but Harry had other ideas. He was already checking his dominoes in a new, eternal game, far away.

That very evening also saw the passing of Pitma Capone, so called in deference to his affection for the national plebeian headgear, the skip-bunneted Glasgow-Italian equivalent of his famous Homburg-hatted distant relative of Chicago fame. He had been a second-generation Italian whose father had slipped off an emigration ship sailing from Italy to Canada, which en route had called into the Clyde for repairs. Pitma's father had gone on to become a successful and respected businessman in Glasgow and had still found time to produce two sons. Both brothers also went into business, one in Glasgow, the other in Edinburgh. Unfortunately, along the way, they had both become involved in various rackets.

Rivals on numerous occasions had tried to dispose of Pitma, just as he had similarly attempted to reduce his competition. His competitors were therefore surprised, and delighted, when they heard he had passed on after choking on his daily plate of spaghetti carbonara.

And that was how Maria Zarotti, Harry Dingwall and Pitma Capone came to be resting in Jammy's Room of Repose, all at the same time.

+   +   +

'Dae ye know, Jammy,' mused Laughing-Boy. 'ah wis jist thinking.'

'Ah chust thought ah could smell wood burning,' observed Jammy.

'Naw, naw, be serious for a minute, Jammy. Ah wis jist thinking that we are a vital concern. We're jist as necessary as aw they meenisters and priests that conduct weddings. In fact, ah think funerals are mair important than weddings. A person can have umpteen weddings, but they only get wan funeral,' he concluded.

'True, true,' said a thoughtful Jammy. 'Though at a wedding ye can at least smell yer ain flooers.'

The entire staff of Stewarts Undertakers were in the dark wood and leather surroundings of Jammy's office, a room with a wooden floor which was partly covered with a stained and threadbare carpet. Twenty years worth of cigar smoke yellowed the ceiling and clung to just about everything. Dog-eared back issues of *Funeral Director's Monthly* cluttered the shelves. A painting, allegedly of Jammy's great grandfather fishing in Skye, gathered dust behind Jammy's desk.

Jammy pushed back his chair and stood up. 'Right everyone,' he started, 'we're in fur a busy couple o' days. We've got a full hoose jist noo. Chust the way ah like it, as you know. So you'll aw need tae be on yer toes as we have back-tae-back funerals. Dae ye hear that, Rip Van Winkle?' he demanded of his dozy driver. 'Nae going tae sleep while yer sitting in the limo.'

'Ah hear ye loud an' clear, Jammy,' yawned Rip.

'Right, then. Noo listen, we've hired a couple o' taxis to help oot wi' the number of family mourners at Maria Zarotti's cremation. There should be a big crowd. The service at the church is ten o'clock, and at the crematorium at eleven. By the way, Rip, how's Lazarus behaving?'

'Started first time this morning, Jammy.'

'Aye, well let's hope he behaves himsel' the day.'

Lazarus did run smoothly that day, in fact most things did. As expected, Maria Zarotti's funeral was well attended. She had been a popular figure in the area, always with a cheery word for her faithful clientele. The Zarotti family was big. Cousins appeared from all parts of Scotland. The church was full of people wishing to pay their last respects. The singing was lusty, with tears shed as the priest recounted Maria's many acts of kindnesses in the community. Everybody agreed it was a fine funeral service, a suitable send off for the well-liked Italian-Scot.

The crematorium was packed too for what again proved to be a moving service. Lazarus purred along, delivering Maria on time to both places.

At the end of the day, Jammy and his team were tired, but satisfied with their day's work. Everything had gone as planned and Jammy retired to his office to catch up on paperwork.

It was around five o'clock, just as GFT was about to leave for the day, that the phone call came.

'Stewarts the Undertakers. Can we be of assistance to youse?' GFT responded.

A gruff voice said, 'The boss wants tae talk tae your boss.' GFT buzzed through to Jammy.

'Good evening, Stewarts the Undertakers here,' said Jammy. 'How can ah help ye.'

'Haud on. Ah getta the boss,' came the reply.

It seemed an age before another voice was heard. This one was deep, powerful and threatening.

'Ah'm comin' tae see ma brother tomorrow.'

Jammy sat up, any tiredness all gone, now alert and concerned. This could only be 'Second Chance' Capone. Only, as everyone knew, 'Second Chance' never gave anyone a second chance.

'Everything is fine, Mister Capone, kind sur. We have your brother in a fine Scots pine coffin, the very finest. Och, and the burial is tomorrow, eh, at two at Rutherglen cemetery.

'Listen to me, Stewart. I am very sure my brother is in a fine Scottish pine coffin. That is no' important. We are an old Sicilian family. You should understand that it is essential that as the elder brother I visit him. I need to kiss my dead kinsman goodbye. It's an old Sicilian tradition, understand? It is extremely important to the Family.'

'Absolutely, absolutely, kind sur,' twittered Jammy. 'That's whit we are here fur, to keep the family happy. Whit time will you arrive tomorrow, Mister Capone?'

'We will be at your funeral establishment at noon precisely.

Ah like perfection. Understand?' he replied, a menacing edge to
his voice.

'No problem, kind sur,' gasped Jammy nervously, but the
line was already dead.

'Second Chance' Capone, the gangster, coming to Stewarts!
Jammy had only ever seen 'Second Chance' in newspaper
photographs, coming out of courtrooms where the case against
him had inexplicably been found 'Not Proven'. Jammy was
suddenly conscious of his sweaty palms and palpitating heart.

But what was there to worry about? he reasoned. Absolutely
nothing! Word might even get around, and Stewarts the
Undertakers get more business in the future from some of the
Glasgow 'Boys'. Still, he felt apprehensive?

'Happy!' he shouted. 'Get in here right noo, wid ye.'

A surly looking Happy-Harry peeked round the door.

'Happy,' instructed Jammy, in a somewhat throaty voice.
'Go in and check on Pitma Capone. Make sure everything is
tickety-boo. His brother, 'Second-Chance Capone, is coming in
tae see him at twelve o'clock tomorrow.'

'Right, Jammy. Ah'll dae it right noo. Then ah'll be away.
We've had a busy day the day.'

'Good lad, Happy. Just do me a wee favour wid ye, and let
me know everything is okay afore ye go?' added Jammy, feeling a
slight premonitory spasm of anxiety in his lower back.

Jammy tried to resume his paperwork, but he could still
hear the menace in 'Second Chance's' voice. 'Widnae like tae get
on the wrong side o' yon, indeedy no',' Jammy murmured to
himself.

Suddenly his office door crashed open. Happy stood, his
face a mask of terror.

'Whit is it, man?' asked Jammy anxiously. 'Ye look like
'Crazy Horse' MacGonigal's ghost.'

'Oh Goad, Jammy!' stuttered Happy. 'We musta cremated
Pitma the day. We musta mixed up Mrs Zarotti and him. We've
still got Mrs Zarotti. She's lying in Pitma's coffin.'

'Whit! Don't be saft. That cannae be right! Let me see!'
blabbed Jammy, and he dashed passed the stricken Happy.

But there, lying in the Glasgow gangster's coffin looking
peaceful and content, was Maria Zarotti.

'Aw, naw. How in the name o' the wee man did this happen? Heavens above, ah'm deid, deid, deid and mair deid, that's whit ah am, indeedy ah am!' wailed a despairing Jammy.

'Jammy, we've been that busy,' pleaded Happy. 'it's just a wee mistake. Mister 'Second Chance' will understand, I'm sure. Efter aw, his brother's deid onyways. We could collect the ashes the morn and give them tae him when he comes in. Pit them in a really nice wee urn.'

'Happy! Are you oot o' yer skull, man?' Jammy shook Happy by the lapels. 'Do you no' understand? This is the end o' all of us. Stewart Undertakers is finished. They Sicilian gangsters have wiped oot generations fur less. When's the last plane for Bolivia the night? It's ma only hope. Mind you,' he added. 'ah hear they fellows will follow you wherever you go. The world is a dangerous place, ye know. It isnae safe onymore tae be alive. Och, why did ah ever leave Skye, ah ask ye, indeedy ah do. Why?' By the time he'd finished Happy's teeth were rattling.

Jammy was distraught, panicking. He sat in his office, head in hands, mind racing. The business he had successfully built up was just about to go under. In fact, he would be going under, too. Oh, what was to be done? There was no hope. Not a glimmer. He was doomed!

Happy slumped in the chair opposite him, if possible looking gloomier than ever. In desperation he said, 'Can we no' maybe pit a wig on Maria Zarotti and make her look like Pitma?'

'Dinny be daft, Happy. She's a woman. He'd notice the difference, ya daft bampot!' exclaimed Jammy. But the wheels in his brain started to grind, and he suddenly exclaimed, 'Hey! Maybe yer oan tae something right enough, Happy. When's Sergeant Dingwall's funeral?'

'Three o'clock tomorrow. Why?'

'Well, he's a man, no' a woman,' explained Jammy, stating the obvious. 'Whit happened tae Pitma Capone's claes? Have we gie'd them back tae the family yet?' asked Jammy.

'Pitma's claes are in a wee case ready to be picked up,' Happy told him.

'Right, get them oot. Pit them on Sergeant Dingwall. It's oor only hope.'

'But Sergeant Dingwall's got a beard, Jammy.'

'Then shave it aff him, quick, man!'

That night Jammy couldn't sleep. He tossed and turned, going over and over in his mind various scenarios, and planning escape routes out the back of the parlour. He would have one of the cars sitting there. He would go and live on a wee deserted island in the Western Isles. Surely they Mafia thugs wouldn't follow him there? It would be too cold and rainy for them, he rationalized.

Jammy was back at the parlour at the crack of dawn. He peeked in at Harry Dingwall, now dressed in Pitma's clothes. The jacket had just about made it on the shoulders. Harry Dingwall had liked his food, and it showed. 'Och, dear heavens,' wailed Jammy. ''Second-chance' wull see in a minute this isnae his brother.' In desperation he turned the Room of Repose's dimmer switch to its lowest setting.

Back in his office Jammy had breakfast; a large whisky. His shaking hands only just managed to raise it to his lips. As the whisky hit his empty stomach he began to feel a bit better. Och, there would be no trouble at all, at all, he reassured himself. 'Second-Chance' would chust assume his brother had put on weight. Might even congratulate Jammy for looking after Pitma so well.

But as time passed, the doubts returned. He found himself paralysed by fear. 'A Scicilian kiss,' he moaned. 'Well, ah'll be getting' mair than chust a 'Glasgow kiss'.'

The hands on the office clock crawled round. He checked it several times against his pocket watch, but it was going. Eventually the hands approached twelve o'clock. High noon! thought Jammy. Noo' ah know how Gary Cooper felt. At least he had a gun. Then another thought struck him. Probably 'Second-Chance' would have one. Well, at least it wid be quick.

The intercom on his desk buzzed. In a tremulous voice GFT informed him there were three gentlemen to see him in the foyer. Jammy stood, fixed his tie with some effort, and opened the door. Three large men dressed in dark suits faced him. The middle one, wearing shades, was 'Second-Chance' Capone.

'Where's ma brither?' he growled.

'This way, Mister Capone, kind sur,' trembled Jammy, leading the way to the Room of Repose.

As they entered the room 'Second-Chance' was overcome by emotion, and was having to cling to one of his gorillas as he stumbled towards his brother's coffin.

'Ah'll leave ye alane wi' ye brither, kind sur,' Jammy said, and went back to the foyer, where the remaining thug gave him a menacing glance. 'Ah'll be in ma office,' he informed the man, 'if yer boss wants tae see me.' The thought then crossed his mind that it would probably be better if the killing took place there. After all, it would save messing up the rest of the funeral parlour.

The whisky bottle was once more removed from the desk drawer. Jammy sat, hands clasped in prayer, sweat pouring down his face, eyes closed. He was resigned to his fate.

Suddenly, the door swung opened. 'Second-Chance' Capone stood, tears streaming down his cheeks. 'Ye've done a fine job on ma brither, Mister Stewart,' he sobbed. 'Although ah still cannae see since the acid attack, ah could smell the cigar smoke fae his old smoking jacket. It fair brought back memories. Ah'll be at the funeral this afternoon. Me and ma boys are away for some lunch noo. Thanks again. The Family wull no' forget this, Mister Stewart.'

' 'Second-Chance' … blind!' thought Jammy. 'Jings, whit a let-aff. Ah'm goin' tae live!' he giggled hysterically. Dashing out to the foyer he found Happy, Laughing-Boy and GFT waiting expectantly. 'Right, you lot. The big man's happy, so ah'm dead happy. Get Sergeant Dingwall back intae his ain coffin. Put Maria Zarotti in Pitma's, and make sure the lids are screwed doon tight. Ah'm sure Pitma widnae object tae an Italian woman in his grave.'

'So, boys and girls, let's get organized,' said Jammy determinedly, rubbing his hands before reaching for a celebration cigar. 'We've a busy day ahead, indeedy we have. Chust imagine though,' he added with a thoughtful smile, 'a big Glesca polis gettin' kissed by the Mafia!'

✚   ✚   ✚

Dead Funnies

'Right, steady lads, take the strain,' instructed Jammy, as they prepared to take the coffin of the deceased from the house.

'Hey, youse!' came a sudden cry from the widow. 'Jist haud on a wee minute. Ye've forgotten his 'gone and dunnit'.'

'Whit's that, madom?'

'His bunnet, of course. He wore it aw the time. Even tae his bed. So he better wear it noo he's 'pan breid'!'

+ + +

Jammy, Happy Harry and Laughing-Boy, all looked out of the parlour window at the passing cortege. It was a funeral by a rival funeral company and comprised two hearses, one containing a magnificent black oak coffin, the other had nothing but wreaths and flowers, both within and on top of the vehicle.

The two hearses were followed by twenty gleaming limousines, all containing extremely, well-dressed mourners.

'Noo,' observed an impressed Jammy. 'that's whit ah call livin'!'

+ + +

A dignified gentleman was in the office seeing Jammy about the arrangements for his wife's forthcoming funeral. 'She was actually my second wife, Mister Stewart,' he explained. 'My first marriage was terminated by death.'

'And by whose death was it terminated, kind sur?' asked Jammy, somewhat unthinkingly.

+ + +

'Have you ever had a near-death experience, Jammy?' asked Tottie the barman.

'Och, ah had something much worse than that once, Tottie. Sure ah was nearly married wance!'

+ + +

Jammy and Laughing-Boy were busy preparing to put the deceased gentleman into his coffin, when the bedroom door opened and in came the widow.

'Could ye put this in the coffin wi' him?' she asked, producing a life jacket. 'Ye see, he wis a keen yachtsman.'

'Did he drown, madom?' asked Jammy.

'Naw,' replied the widow, 'he just seemed tae keel over.'

✦ ✦ ✦

'So, Jammy, really all you do is assist people on their final journey from the 'cradle to the grave'?' asked Tottie.

'Och, that ah do, indeedy ah do,' replied the undertaker thoughtfully. 'Though some posh folks on the South Side like the expression, 'womb to the tomb'. As long as ah'm makin' money oot it they can call it 'erection tae resurrection' fur aw ah care!'

✦ ✦ ✦

The widow was going over, with Jammy, the details of her husband's forthcoming funeral. Finally she added, 'Ah wid like a special bit o' music played at the end.'

'Was this a favourite piece o' him himsel'?' asked Jammy.

'Naw, naw. It's ma ain idea, really,' she replied. 'Ye see he wis a double-glazing salesman, so ah wid like '*Knockin' on Heaven's Door*'."

✦ ✦ ✦

'An' did he have ony last words, madom?' asked Jammy.

'Aye. He said, 'Ah don't know how that wee shop on the corner can make any profit selling they corn beef tins at sixpence each'.'

✦ ✦ ✦

'A freen o' mines wance stopped puttin' oan weight, stopped smokin', went teetotal and went right aff the lassies, aw at the same time,' observed a straight- faced Jammy to Tottie. 'Mind you, ah gied him himsel' a lovely funeral.'

✦ ✦ ✦

When Jammy and Rip got to the tenement flat, they found the body of the husband on the bedroom floor. He was wearing pink pyjamas.

'Dae ye like his pink pyjamas?' asked the widow.

'Well, madom,' replied Jammy, somewhat taken aback, 'they are, er, different. Noo, dae ye want him tae wear a shroud or a suit?''

'Naw, ah want him buried in these pyjamas.'

'Och, right ye are then,' replied a surprised Jammy. 'It's really of little consequence efter aw, madom. But is there any particular reason why you want himsel' in his pyjamas?'

'Aye,' replied the woman, 'Two minutes afore he had his heart attack, he said, 'An' see they pink pyjamas ye got me fur ma birthday, ye can jist take them back tae the shop. Ye widnae get me wearin' them o'er ma dead boady!''

✦ ✦ ✦

Jammy stood at the entrance to the crematorium chapel. The mourners were all seated apart from one latecomer who had just appeared. The fellow was dressed in an ill-fitting black suit, the top button of his shirt undone, black tie hanging loose. Going up to Jammy he asked, 'Which side dae ah sit, pal? Ah'm wi' the deceased.'

✦ ✦ ✦

'And are there any other requests you would like to make regarding your husband's funeral?' Jammy asked the widow.

'Aye. He wis in a Scottish Country dance band, and he always said he wanted his auld fiddle to go with him in his coffin,' replied the widow. 'Is that alright, Mister Stewart?'

'No problem whatsoever, madom, though ah'm assuming it's no' a Stradivarius,' replied Jammy. 'Anyway, it's chust a blessing he didnae play the accordion!'

+   +   +

GFT popped her head around Jammy's office door. 'There's a man here tae see you,' she stated. 'He says it's no' about arranging a funeral, but he won't tell me whit it is.'

'Och, jist tell him tae come in here onyways, GFT,' said Jammy. 'Ah'll see whit it's aw aboot.'

The man, wearing a serious, troubled face, was probably in his early forties, Jammy reckoned. He entered, reluctantly sitting across the desk from Jammy.

'Can Stewart Undertakers be of some assistance to you, kind sur?' enquired Jammy.

'Maybe,' came a hesitant reply. 'Ye see, ah'm thinkin' o' gettin' a divorce.'

'Och, sorry to hear that,' Jammy said in his usual funereal manner. 'So, how can we be of help?'

'Aye, well,' said the man, unable to meet Jammy's eyes. 'Ye see ah need some sort o' verification on a situation.'

'Well, kind sur, ah will try. But you will understaun that we never disclose personal details regarding our customers. No indeedy.'

'Ah understaun that. But ye see it's like this,' said the man, clearly struggling to communicate his problem. 'Two nights ago ma wife an' her pal went oot fur a drink. If ye ask me they had a pile o' the stuff. Anyways, ma wife's story is that on the way back hame they were passing the cemetery and were dying fur a pee. So they managed to get o'er the wa', but didnae hae ony toilet paper, so they say they just, er ... improvised. Mister Stewart, the lang and the short o' it is that ah need ye tae verify something aboot a recent funeral ma wife claims must have taken place.'

'Och, if ah can, indeedy ah will,' replied the now intrigued Jammy.

'See this is the problem, Mister Stewart. Ma wife arrived hame wi a wee card stickin' tae her bum that read, 'We will always remember you – 'The Boys at the Fire Station'.'

+   +   +

'See auld Fred over there,' remarked Jammy, nodding to the corner of the lounge bar, 'Husnae two halfpennies tae rub the gether. Och, and the smell! Disnae wash fae wan day's morn tae the next.'

'He'll end up in a pauper's grave, that yin,' observed Tottie.

'Aye, an' if he does, the pauper will probably complain.'

+   +   +

The widow was in the parlour, promptly paying the bill for her husband's funeral in order to qualify for a small discount.

'Was everything to your liking, madom?' asked Jammy.

'Jist wonderful. It wis a grand funeral,' she replied. 'It's jist a shame though he couldnae o' bin there tae see it!'

+   +   +

'Ye see, Mister Stewart,' said the gentleman sitting in Jammy's office to arrange his own pre-paid funeral. 'Ah don't know whit it is, but ah seem tae upset a lot o' people aw the time. Naebuddy really likes me.'

'Come, come, kind sur,' extolled Jammy. 'I'm sure ye must have some friends.'

'Nut one. Even ma wife and ma dug have left me. So, ah don't expect too many folks at ma funeral when ma time comes. Onybuddy that's there will only be because they're glad tae see the back o' me. So, ah don't want ony cheery hymns or anything like that. Jist an auld Scots sang they wull aw hate tae sing.'

'And whit wid that be,' asked Jammy.

The wan that goes, '*Wull ye no' come back again*'!'

+   +   +

When Jammy got to the old folks' home, the elderly lady was laid out on the bed in a spare room.

'Always sat in the chair next to the fire in the lounge, she did,' observed the matron. 'In fact, that's where she died.'

'Och, ah can tell,' commented Jammy, 'she fair looks like death warmed up!'

+   +   +

Jammy was manoeuvring the coffin in the bedroom of a first floor flat, when he fell backwards, right through the window. Happy Harry rushed to the window and looked out onto the street.

'Is he aw right?' enquired Rip anxiously.

'Och, aye. 'Dead Jammy' as usual,' joked Happy Harry. 'Lazarus is sittin' just below the window, so he's jist fallen on his 'earse!'

+   +   +

Jammy was at the doctor, complaining of arthritis.

'If you don't want to be a little stiff, then you should take vitamin C each day,' advised the practitioner.

'Don't tell any mair o' yer patients that, dochter. By chove, ah need aw the stiffs ah can get ma hauns on.'

+   +   +

5

'Dead Jammy' and the two wives

GFT opened Jammy's office door, and apprehensively seated herself on the edge of the chair across from her employer. Always a bad sign. She sighed, glancing nerviously at the sheaf of forms in her hand.

Jammy looked up, expecting the usual moans about something or other. Slowly, he went through his extended ritual of lighting a cigar, then taking a long draw in order to add to the rancid haze of smoke already circling the room. Then he said, 'Can you no' see ah'm preoccupied at the minute, GFT?'

'Wid ye like a cup o' coffee, Jammy?' asked the receptionist, unexpectedly.

'Ah don't like the sound o' this, GFT, indeedy ah don't,' said Jammy, now sitting bolt upright and looking at her directly. 'Ah've never known ye afore tae come intae ma office an' offer tae make me a cuppa.'

GFT looked uncertainly at the funeral director. He had never seen her so subdued.

'You know how you were off yesterday, Jammy, seeing the builders aboot the extension tae yer hoose,' she began. 'Well, a wee

wumman came in and made arrangements for her husband's funeral.'

'So, whit's the problem, GFT? When they stop coming in tae arrange funerals, it's then we have a problem, indeedy we do.'

'Well,' said GFT, continuing with her tale. 'ah couldnae help but notice that her man wis born on Saint Valentine's Day, the fourteenth o' February. And another thing. The wee wuman said she was shocked that he had died so young. Apparently he took care o' himsell. In fact, he wis a vegetarian.'

'That means there's bound tae be a big turnup at the funeral,' quipped Jammy, blowing cigar smoke high in the air.

'Listen. Be serious fur a minute, Jammy!' remonstrated GFT. 'Here's the problem. There's another lady ootside the noo, wantin' tae bury her man, and ah'm sure it's the same vegetarian fella as yesterday. This wan wis born on the same Saint Valentine's Day.'

'Ye mean, this fella might've been a bigamist?'

'Could be. Whit are we gonny dae, Jammy? We cannae bury the same body twice. In fact it's worse than that. Wan wants him buried and the ither wants him cremated. An' it's a 'mixed grill' tae. Wan says he was Catholic, the other Church of Scotland. Anyway, is there no' a penalty for bigamy?'

'Och, indeedy, GFT,' smiled Jammy. 'Two mothers-in-laws.'

'Very droll, Jammy! But seriously whit are we tae dae? She's waitin' ootside. Ah'm awfa worried aboot this,' GFT concluded.

'Let me handle the situation, GFT. It obviously calls for a bit o' executive intervention,' said Jammy in his best officious manner. He rose, looked in the ornamental mirror on the office wall, straightened a few wisps of hair, and went to the door.

'Naw, haud oan, Jammy. There's something else ah must tell ye,' said GFT, looking guilty. Ludicrous was just about to give way to surreal. 'Ye see it's even mair complicated. Tae tell ye the truth the widow ootside is actually ma cousin, oan ma mither's side. That's why she wants tae use Stewarts the Undertakers. So, Jammy, could you do me a big favour? Don't tell the polis aboot any bigamy, sure ye won't? It wid bring great shame tae oor family. We're awfa close. Ah'm confident ye'll find some way roon this situation. You're guid at this type o' thing.'

'Guid at this type o' thing! Fur heaven's sake, GFT, ah've

never had such a situation in all ma years as an undertaker. It's ma duty as a member o' the Funeral Director's Association to report such a crime, indeedy it is.'

'Please, please, Jammy.' pleaded GFT, 'help ma family oot. Ah'm wan o' yer longest serving employees. Anyways,' she added cunningly. 'ye must remember, when it comes tae this business, ah know where aw the bodies are buried.'

'Ah hope ah misunderstand you, GFT,' replied Jammy, his eyes narrowing, and his tone hardening, 'an' that's not a hint o' blackmail in yer voice, indeedy ah do.'

'Naw, naw, Jammy,' replied GFT, in panic. 'Sure ah'm a loyal servant o' yours!'

'Aye, well, maybe so. Noo, let me think. Chust let me see whit ah kin dae. Ah'm no' promising ye anything though. When it's two faiths in a marriage, ah mean a 'mixed grill', death can get complicated enough. But two wives o' different faiths and wan boady! Some deid folks are gey careless, if ye ask me. It's us poor undertakers that have tae fix things. Anyways, whit's this wuman's name?'

'She's a Mrs Smith. The other wuman is a Mrs Broon.'

'Well, ah'll say wan thing fur this philanderer. He liked tae keep it simple.' And with that observation Jammy opened the office door.

'Good morning, madom,' said Jammy politely, seeing a well-dressed lady standing at the reception desk. 'Perhaps you would care to come into the office, and ah can complete the details on Mister Smith's funeral.'

With the widow duly seated, Jammy went into his usual routine. 'First of all, madom, thank you for choosing oor establishment for your spouse's arrangements.'

'Well, ye see, Mister Stewart,' replied the lady, 'ma cousin, Miss Teenan, works fur you, as you probably know.'

'Och, indeedy, a faithful wuman o'er many years,' replied Jammy. 'Noo, how lang were ye married tae Mister Smith?'

'Fifteen years almost tae the day. Ah've goat tae tell ye, Mister Stewart, he wis a loving husband. Even though he was away for a fortnight at a time working on the rigs in the North Sea, he wis a solid, family man. Always reliable. Virile too, though when he came hame he wis aye fair exhausted. Took him a few days tae get his breath back. Ah'm gonnae miss him, Mister Stewart, ah can tell ye.' And she began to sob.

'There, there, madom,' said Jammy sympathetically, giving her a tissue. 'Stewarts the Undertakers will take good care o' you and yer man.' Though privately he could see no way out of the dilemma.

'And where would Mister Smith's body be at present?' he asked.

'Why, sure he's here, in yer ain funeral parlour. Ma man wis delivered yesterday. Ye see he died when he wis away oan the rig. Ah must say his employers have been awfa good makin' aw the arrangements, and such like. They even sent ma poor man directly tae you.' And again she was engulfed in tears.

'Ah know it's a difficult time fur ye, madom,' continued Jammy, 'but ah wis wondering whit ye had in mind fur the funeral.'

'Ah think jist the crematorium, an' a wee tea in the hoose efterwards. We're Presbyterian, and oor minister wull be happy tae tak the service, even if Mister Smith didnae go o'er often.'

'Right then, madom,' said Jammy. 'You just leave Stewarts tae make the arrangements. Ah'll gae ye a wee phone call when ah have the time arranged wi' the crematorium.' Then, with a nod of his head and a handshake, Mrs Smith was hastily shown the door.

'Right, GFT,' said Jammy sternly to his receptionist. 'You an' me need tae have a serious chat. In ma office! Noo!'

With the door tightly closed, Jammy started. 'This is a gey monstrous situation ye've goat Stewarts intae, GFT, indeedy it is. We could get thrown oot the Association, you know. Nae mair conferences fur me in Peebles. All oor futures are at stake here, including yours! This could be the final nail in oor coffin.' He peered meaningfully at his receptionist. 'Noo, tell me, this Mrs Broon who wis in yesterday, what were her arrangements?'

'Well,' began a subdued GFT, 'Mrs Broon was originally going tae have the body hame, but has noo decided tae leave it here tae be delivered to the church the night afore the funeral. Father O'Brien is taking the service, then on tae Rutherglen cemetery.'

'Ah chust don't know how you've got me intae this, GFT?'

continued Jammy. 'Regardless o' whit ye say, it's blackmail, that's whit it is.'

'Naw, naw, Jammy, Mister Stewart, sir, that's no' true. The problem is, that ah've such a guid memory fur detail.' the cunning look was back on her face. 'And remember, it's helped you oot on many an occasion, sure it has?'

'Mmmmm,' murmered an unsure Jammy, a distant look coming into his eyes. He fairly enjoyed aw they conferences. Ye got a great selection o' whiskies, indeedy you did. But it didn't matter how GFT put it, it wis blackmail, pure and simple. Well, there had to be a solution to the situation, but what?

✦   ✦   ✦

Mister Smith's funeral at the crematorium went well. The minister was an old pro, knew his stuff. Talked about Mister Smith's love of his family and his great passion for Glasgow Rangers.

The following morning Mister Smith's ashes were duly collected at the crematorium by Rip Van Winkle, put in an ornamental urn, and delivered to Mrs Smith. Although overcome with grief, she placed them with great pride on top of her piano.

Later, at Mister Brown's funeral, Father O'Brien talked about Mister Brown's love of his family and his great passion for Glasgow Celtic. Apart from Mrs Brown, another three unknown widows turned up at the cemetery, all dabbing at their eyes and looking at each other suspiciously.

'By chove,' observed Rip Van Winkle to Jammy as they drove back from the cemetery. 'That fella must have fairly got around. And Father O' Brien said he had been a solid family man, a right brick.'

'Well, Father O'Brien wis nearly right aboot him being a brick, Rip,' observed Jammy with a wink. 'Though noo he's twenty-eight o' them!'

✦   ✦   ✦

Dead Funnies

'Ma man worked for Glasgow Corporation, you know,' explained the widow.

'Och, ah see, madom,' said Jammy. 'And may ah ask where he died?'

'Well, that wis the funny thing aboot it, Mister Stewart. It came as a terrible shock tae me because he died at his work. The doctor said that he jist passed away in his sleep.'

+   +   +

'Any requests regarding cord bearers at your burial?' Jammy asked the local businessman, who was arranging his pre-paid funeral.

'Just one, Mister Stewart. Ah would like the manager of the Bank up the road tae be one of them. He's let me down for nearly twenty years, so he may as well finish the job.'

+   +   +

GFT rang through to Jammy's office. 'Mister Stewart,' she said in her usual officious manner, 'there are three young gentlemen here to see you about their mother's demise.'

In the foyer Jammy found the three young men, all in their early twenties. It transpired that their widowed mother had left instructions she wanted Stewarts to handle her funeral.

Jammy duly took them into his office, and went over the various details. 'Wan thing, Mister Stewart,' said the eldest son.'We've a request o' oor ain. Some music that we want played in the crematorium. It's actually a rock number. Ye see, we're aw big fans o' Jim Morrison and the *Doors*.'

'No problem whatsoever, kind sur' said Jammy. 'We get all sorts of requests, you know. And what is it that ye would like played?'

'*Light My Fire!*'

+   +   +

The stranger introduced himself as the nephew of the deceased.

'So, your firm is doing ma uncle's burial tomorrow?'

'Och, that wid be correct, yes indeedy,' replied Jammy.

'Well, ah promised ma uncle ah wid pour a bottle o' his favourite malt over his grave. Unfortunately, Mister Stewart, ah've goat tae leave tonight fur two years in Saudi. Ah wonder if you could dae it fur me?' he asked, producing a bottle.

'Och, ah wid be honoured tae dae it, chust fur you an' yer uncle,' replied Jammy.

'Great,' said the nephew. 'An' nae running it through yer kidneys afore ye dae it, mind!'

'How did yer day go?' asked Tottie, as he poured a double for the undertaker.

'No' bad,' replied Jammy. 'Though at the funeral o' an' auld spinster, the minister fell right intae the grave on tae the coffin.'

'Och, well,' said Tottie. 'At least the auld spinster finally had a man on tap o' her!'

+   +   +

The young man was in the parlour arranging his grandmother's funeral.

'Right then, kind sur,' said Jammy, 'we'll be able to do your gran's funeral on Friday.'

'But that's five days away,' complained the grandson. 'Can we no' have it on Wednesday?'

'A'm very sorry, kind sur,' Jammy explained. 'But we're awfu' busy the noo. It's been that bad flu, ye know.'

'Ah, weel,' replied the grandson, 'fair enough. But if ye get a cancellation maybe you could give me a ring.'

+   +   +

'If someone dies in their sleep, Jammy,' asked Tottie the barman, 'do they know it when they get up in the morning?'

'Whit!' exclaimed Jammy. There was no answer to that!

+   +   +

'You'll no' believe this, Jammy,' said Rip Van Winkle. 'Ah hope it's no' an omen. When we were at Linn Crematorium the day, ah pit ma haun in ma overcoat fur ma hankie, an' oot came the wee ticket ah goat this morning when ah wis in the supermarket getting the wife some fish. It says, 'Your Turn Next'!'

+   +   +

'The trouble is,' ventured Tottie the barman, 'ma wife wull probably live furever.'

'Is she hersell a very healthy type, then?' asked Jammy

'Naw especially. It's just that she reckons she's nothing tae wear apart fae dresses she widnae be seen deid in!'

+   +   +

Jammy was with a family who were paying their 'last respects' to their father in the funeral parlour. 'Och,' observed Jammy, 'ah know it must be a difficult time fur you good folks, but just remember that what you see before ye today is chust the shell, indeedy it is. The nut has gone to a better place.'

49

+   +   +

'What occupation was he himself, madom?' Jammy asked the widow.

'Oh, he wis a window cleaner.'

'And when did he stop working.'

'Aboot half-way doon!'

+ + +

'Ah wis thinking o' supplementin' ma income, Jammy,' said Tottie the barman. 'They pay ye tossers in here. Ah see there's a part-time job at Rutherglen cemetery as a gravedigger. Maybe you could put in a good word for me?'

'Och, if ye like,' said Jammy wi a smile. 'but ah must tell ye that ah heard they jist want somebuddy tae fill in.'

+ + +

'We should get get rid o' auld Lazarus. That hearse keeps breakin' doon at the most awkward moments,' complained Happy Harry. 'Every time we pass a scrapyard it gets homesick.'

'Och, you could be right, Happy,' replied Jammy. 'Jist let me look in the Funeral Director Monthly magazine an' see if there are ony second-hand wans fur sale.'

Looking through the magazine Jammy suddenly exclaimed. 'Aye, here's wan, Happy, an' it looks as though we might get a wee bit o' business alang wi it. It says, 'For sale, British Leyland hearse -1957. Body in good condition'.'

+ + +

When Jammy, Happy Harry, and Laughing-Boy all got to the flat they found Sammy sitting in a chair. It was clear the old fellow had been reading his paper, and had just passed peacefully away. Unfortunately rigor mortis had already set in. 'Right,' instructed Jammy. 'efferything is quiet outside the noo, naebuddy aboot, so we'll jist carry him oot and stick him in the back o' the car.'

Sammy was duly lifted out between Happy Harry and Laughing-Boy, and 'helped' down the stairs into the back seat of the car, where he sat between the two undertakers back to the parlour.

The following week Jammy was in the *Pigs and Whistles* having a friendly dram. Tottie the barman turned to Jammy and said, 'Hey, ah hear old Sammy died. Did you dae the funeral?'

'That ah did, Tottie.'

'A'm no' surprised he's deid,' observed Tottie. 'Ma wife saw him recently in the backseat o' a car, and apparently he didnae look aw that grand.'

+   +   +

'Mister Stewart, can ye come roon tae the hoose? Ma man's deid,' said the voice on the phone.

'Och, dear-a-dear-a-dear,' commiserated Jammy. 'Have you phoned the doctor yet?'

'Nae need. This wan's face looks like he's jist given the pallbearers the slip!'

+   +   +

'He wis a dentist, ye ken,' said Happy Harry, looking down at the deceased.

'Och, aye, and he'll soon be filling his last cavity,' observed Jammy.

+   +   +

The deceased had died in a tenement flat in a less than fashionable district of Glasgow.

'Excuse me, Mister Stewart,' said the widow, coming into the bedroom where Jammy and Laughing-Boy were busy screwing down the lid of the coffin. 'Ah want a word wi that wan afore he goes.' Laughing-Boy looked at Jammy who shrugged, and started to unscrew the lid.

'Listen you,' began the widow, addressing her dead husband. 'Jist so youse know. Ah want wan o' they big mansions in heaven. An' see if it's no' goat an inside toilet, there'll be hell tae pay when ah get there!'

+   +   +

The organist at the crematorium was upstairs in the balcony, in a position where only the officiating 'man of the cloth' could see him. The organist and Jammy saw each other often, and tended to swap wee funny stories. Both had the same kind of unfortunate humour.

One day, a new minister from out of town was taking a funeral. At the last verse of the final hymn, just before the committal, the organist whipped out a pair of large plastic ears, and put them on as he played.

On seeing this, the minister had great difficulty in refraining from laughter. However at the beginning of the final committal, he informed the mourners, 'Ear we go to send the deceased to the earafter.' He then had to stop and compose himself, before continuing.

+   +   +

'Och,' philosophised Happy Harry, 'ye never know the minute, dae ye? It's better tae live every day as though it wis yer last.'

'Och, ah tried that wance when ah wis a teenager,' replied Jammy, 'an' ma faither wouldnae let me oot again fur a month!'

+   +   +

The family stood around the coffin in Stewart's parlour paying their last respects. An aunt remarked to the widow. 'Ah've goat tae say, Mattie. He looks awfa healthy.'

'Aye, so he should dae. He left me alane in the hoose every night and went oot joggin'.'

+   +   +

'Huv ye goat tae lie doon tae die?' asked Tottie the barman.

'Och, nuttatall,' replied Jammy. 'In fact ye could be in the middle o' sippin' a dram.'

'Well, ye had better get that wan doon ye fast jist in case, Jammy. Being a teuchter ye widnae want tae leave ony!'

+   +   +

The coffin was just about to leave the house, when the son shouted, 'Stoap, Mister Stewart! Haud oan a minute. That book ah gaed ye tae haud up ma fether's chin is a library book. It wid cost a fortune in fines. Could you take the lid aff a minute and use this auld Bible?'

+   +   +

Jammy was in the pub. 'Hey, Jammy, whit a day ah've had,' exclaimed Tottie. 'Ah nearly got killed twice crossing the road.'

Jammy gave him a thoughtful look. 'Och, Tottie, man. Wance wid o' been enough fur me.'

+   +   +

6

'Dead Jammy' and the new employee

It seemed like only yesterday that Arthur had been at the 'wee school'. Then there was his first pair of long trousers, the 'big school', the first draw on a Woodbine up a close, the first fumblings behind the school drill hall, his first pint of heavy in the pub, and then his first job. Now he was after another position.

'Ah've come aboot the undertaker's job that's advertised in the buroo,' he informed Jammy.

Jammy eyed him up, a short, skinny lad, with a thin moustache to match.

'Ony experience dealing wi the public? Have ye maybe worked wi the Health Board or such like?' asked the Funeral Director.

'Naw. Ye see, Mister Stewart, ah really wanted tae be a policeman when ah left the school.'

'Ah noble profession, indeed. So are ye a polis at present?'

'Naw, ah couldnae get in. Ma height and ma bowly legs let me doon,' replied Arthur.

'Well, in this job ye can get yer ain back an' let other folks doon,' quipped Jammy. 'So what dae ye work at?'

'Ah've never worked a day in ma life.'

'Never worked a day in yer life?'

'Aye, ah'm a night watchman.'

'A bit o' a comedian, then?'

'Naw, naw, Mister Stewart, ah'm a hard worker. You know, ah can turn ma hand tae anything, an' ah've goat plenty o' common sense. Anyways, is the pay ony good as an undertaker?'

'Good? Of course it's good, indeedy it is. Ah've had the same people working fur me for over twinty years, ah'll have you know. So the money cannae be too bad. And of course there's fringe benefits as well. A free lair or cremation, and twenty percent aff yer ain funeral when yer time comes,' said Jammy. 'Man, half o' Glasgow wid jump at such a generous offer.'

'Does this firm do a lot o' funerals, then?'

'Listen, ah've pit away mair Glaswegians than you've had fish-suppers,' mused Jammy.

'So you're always dead busy?'

'You can say that again, son. Efter aw, that's oor business. Chust so lang as some mad scientist doesnae invent a pill that keeps everybody alive fur ever, then we'll aye have a steady trade, indeedy so.'

'So, dae ah get the job?'

'Well, that depends,' mused a thoughtful Jammy. 'Would you be able to look after oor 'clients'? Ye know, this is a unique line o' business calling for special skills when dealing with the recently departed. Whit hobbies dae ye have?'

'Well, ah like running. Ah'm a harrier ye know. And ah love the pictures, especially 'westerns'. Ah'd have loved to have been a cowboy. Wi' ma legs ah could fit oan a horse nae bother. Ah'm sure ah'll be alright dealing with bodies and the likes. Ah've never seen a dead body afore, apart from in the movies, but ah dinnae believe in ghosts or anything like that.'

'So ye've never heard o' Crazy Horse MacGonigal, the ghost fae Glasgow crematorium?' asked Jammy, his face deadly serious.

'Naw, Mister Stewart. Is that true? Ye've goat tae be at the kiddin', surely?'

'Naw, naw, Arthur. Ah never kid,' replied Jammy, turning slightly to wink at Happy Harry.

'Well, ah'm no' sure ah believe you, Mister Stewart, tae tell you the truth. But ah wid like the job onyways.'

'Ah'll say this fur you, son, you seem dead keen, an' again that's certainly necessary in this trade,' observed Jammy. 'Tell ye whit, we'll gie ye a trial. One month. That's fair, indeedy it is. That way you can find out if the undertaking business is right for you, and we'll find out if you're right for Stewarts, Glasgow's finest undertakers. So, start the morn. But chust remember, this isnae a job. It's a profession. A calling some folks say it is, but really it's an undertaking. We've goat high standards here at Stewarts, indeedy we have.'

✦   ✦   ✦

The following morning Stewart's newest employee was duly set to work. 'Pit that suit on this boady. He's a Mister Munro,' instructed Happy Harry. 'The family brought the suit in. Apparently he wis married in it forty years ago, so his widow wants him buried in it.'

'Jings,' said Arthur, 'he must have kept his clothes in immaculate condition. This suit looks brand new. Anyway, here goes.'

Half an hour later he was back at Happy Harry's side. 'Ah managed tae get the suit oan Mister Munro, but ah had a terrible job. It was far too small. He seems to have put on weight since he wis married. So ah jist cut up the back o' the jacket and the troosers tae get it tae fit him. Ah'm sure Mister Stewart will be pleased that ah used ma common sense.'

Just then GFT appeared with a small case in her hand. 'Mrs Munro just handed this in,' she said. 'She's apparently made a mistake. She gave us her son's new suit instead o' the wan that Mister Munro's to be buried in. Wance ye've pit this auld suit on him, ye've tae pit the other wan in this case. She'll collect it efter the funeral an' have it dry-cleaned.'

Happy Harry looked at a pale-faced Arthur and handed him the case. 'Right, here ye are. Use some o' that common sense ye keep talking aboot an' work this wan oot.'

'But, but ... but how wis ah tae know it wis the wrang suit? Whit dae ye dae in situations like this?'

Happy replied, 'Ah don't know Arthur, ah've never been in a position like this. Ye better go an' have a word wi' the boss. He's the man tae get you oot a jam. That's wan o' the reasons he's called Jammy!'

Jammy was not amused, but understood Arthur's dilemma for had he not himself 'adjusted' many a suit? 'Listen, Arthur,' he said. 'you told me ye had plenty o' common sense. That's why ah hired ye. When ye saw the suit wis new you should have asked yersel', how could the deceased possibly have been married in it forty years ago? Och, well,' he sighed, 'ye'r new tae the trade, ah suppose. We aw have tae learn the hard way. Ye'll chust need tae go oot an' buy a suit, something the same as the wan ye ruined. Tell them tae charge it tae Stewarts. Ah'm ower soft, indeedy ah am.'

'Thank you, Mister Stewart, thanks very much fur being so understanding. Ah'll make sure ah use ma common sense in future.'

'Aye, see you do,' said Jammy.

+   +   +

It was the following day that Jammy was heard by all of his staff cussing away to himself in the toilet of the parlour.

'Whit's the matter wi you this morning, Jammy?' Happy Harry shouted through the door.

'By chove, it's this razor,' came the frustrated voice. 'Ah canny seem tae get a decent shave oot it. It widnae cut butter.'

'Well, it wis fine wi me, Mister Stewart,' chipped in Arthur, 'when ah shaved they two bodies that came in last night.'

The door of the toilet swung slowly open. There stood Jammy, stripped to the waist, holding a towel and with half his face covered in soap. 'Ah'm ah hearing right? You used ma razor tae shave the recently departed? Nae wonder ah cannae get a good shave. We dinnae use personal razors for the bereaved,

we've special razors. Where's this common sense you keep
boasting aboot?'

'Ah'm awfa sorry, Mister Stewart. Ah wis jist trying tae be
helpful.'

'Och, alright. But in future chust you think fur a minute
afore you use that unique brand o' common sense o' yours.'

Later Jammy called Happy Harry over. 'Whit dae ye think
o' oor Arthur? Is he gonnae be any good tae us? That's chust two
days he's been here an' he's yet tae impress me. Seems a bit
harum-scarum cowboy. Dae ye think he's going tae hack it at the
trade, Happy?'

'Ah doubt it, Jammy. Ah hate tae think o' whit he'll get up
tae next.'

'Ah've goat serious reservations masel', Happy, indeedy ah
do. Ah'm afraid that you're chust going tae have tae give him
'The Test'.'

'The 'Test', Jammy? By jingo, it's a while since we last gave
onybuddy 'The 'Test'.'

'Right enough. But it'll show us whit he's made o'. See if his
common sense is up tae anything. If it is, he'll pass. As you know,
Happy, in this game you've got tae react appropriately tae all
situations. So, do your worst! Let's see how it goes.'

The following day the parlour was quiet. There was only one
funeral and just one body brought in, a Mister Wilson. 'Arthur,
put a shroud on Mister Wilson,' instructed Happy Harry. 'At
least it'll fit and you won't have tae cut it up the back.' And he
laughed.

Arthur duly picked out a white shroud from the supplies
cupboard, and made his way to the preparation room where
Mister Wilson's body lay.

The deceased was still clothed in a suit, and Arthur first of
all removed the shoes before unbuttoning the trousers to take
them off. As he bent over to struggle with the final button, Arthur
heard a soft groan. Looking up he was aghast to see Mister
Wilson's eyes slowly open. Then from the corpse's pale lips came
a loud cry of, 'Geronimo!'

'It's 'Crazy Horse'!' screamed the terrified Arthur, hysterically rushing out the door, through the foyer and into the street,
his bowly legs disappearing fast round the nearest corner.

Jammy and Happy Harry watched in hysterics the office window.

'Ah've got tae say, Jammy, Laughing-Boy does a smashing ghost! He could get an Oscar fur that.'

'Aye, dead brilliant he is,' said Jammy. 'An' oor Arthur is obviously a very fir harrier!'

'So, whit dae we dae noo, Jammy, noo that Arthur's failed 'The Test'?' asked Happy Harry.

'Chust go doon tae the broo an' put in another employment notice. But this time put, 'Nae common sense required. And cowboys need not apply!'

+   +   +

Dead Funnies

'An' whit kind o' coffin wid ye like fur yer man, madom?' asked Jammy, showing a catalogue to the widow.

'Huv ye goat wan wi a sort o' 'set-in bed', an' maybe a wee bit o' carpet?'

'By heavens, madom, you've chust got to be at the kidding, indeedy you have! Ah never had a request like that afore.'

'Aye, well ye see, he wis brought up in a single-end.'

+   +   +

The family had all come into the parlour to pay their last respects. They were gathered around the open coffin, making various comments, especially on how well the deceased looked. Indeed, if anything there seemed to be a smile on his face. 'He looks lovely and peaceful, Mister Stewart,' observed the widow, 'don't ye think?'

'Indeedy, madom,' replied Jammy. 'ah don't think it's quite dawned on him yet.'

+   +   +

The lady had come in to see Jammy regarding her father's funeral. 'Mister Stewart,' she confided. 'ma faither had nae money. In fact the only thing ma faither left wis an auld clock.'

'Och, well, chust look on the bright side, madom. At least ye shouldnae have much bother winding up his estate.'

✦   ✦   ✦

Jammy was a confirmed bachelor. However he was really a bit of a ladies' man, if anything preferring the more mature variety. His regular lady friend, Flora MacDonald, was once asked if she would ever marry him.

'Marry a funeral director like Jammy? He's chust efter wan thing. Ma boady!'

✦   ✦   ✦

It was the early hours of Sunday morning. Jammy was awakened during the night by the insistent ringing of the phone.

'Is that Stewart's the Undertakers?' asked an anxious voice.

'Yes, indeedy. Mister Stewart here at your service. Can ah be helping ye?'

'Aye, ma wife has passed away. Ah've goat tae say ah've had an' awful job gettin' a hold o' ye, Mister Stewart. Dae ye no' have a skeleton staff oan at the weekends?

✦   ✦   ✦

He was always more of a fruit and veg man –

'I've come tae make arrangements fur ma man's funeral. He died awfu' sudden like, ' said the lady.

'Fine, madom,' said Jammy. 'Did he himsel' huv ony last requests?'

'Aye, he said, 'Fur heaven's sake, Sadie, pit doon that knife!''

+   +   +

'Well,' said the doctor examining the recently arrived deceased in Jammy's premises. 'Her number is most certainly up.'

'By chove, ye can say that again, doctor,' explained Jammy. She drapped deid after shouting 'hoose' at the bingo last night.'

+   +   +

Jammy was going through various details with the deceased's widow.

'And can ah ask you, madom, whit did he himsel' die o'?'

'Ah really don't know. But ah don't think it wis anything serious.'

+   +   +

'You know, Jammy,' expounded Tottie to the funeral director. 'ah'm really quite a contented man. Ah've had a good life. In fact if the Lord wis tae take me right noo I'd be the happiest man alive.'

'Whit?'

+   +   +

'See when folks die o' natural causes, Jammy,' asked Tottie. 'jist exactly whit does that mean?'

'Well, it means the doctor cannae either spell the medical term for the person's demise, or he chust cannae think o' anything else.'

+   +   +

Angus came to Glasgow from Stornoway many years ago to join the police. After retirement he took to his favourite hobby, the 'water of life'.

When he died his sister came down for the funeral, and insisted on viewing Angus' body at the parlour. So Jammy gave Angus' face a touch-up with a little rouge.

'Och, my o' my,' exclaimed Angus' sister, 'doesn't oor Angus look chust wonderful, noo he's given up the drink!'

✦   ✦   ✦

Rip Van Winkle was in the pub. Someone was droning on about back-seat drivers.

'Ah'll tell ye this,' observed Rip. 'Ah've been driving Jammy Stewart's hearse fur over twinty years, an' ah've never heard even wan word fae behind.'

✦   ✦   ✦

'Ur ye a sports fan at all?' the minister asked Jammy, by way of conversation on the way to Glasgow crematorium. 'Dae ye like the fitba?'

'Naw, yer Holy Reference,' Jammy grinned. 'Though ah really enjoy the cricket, especially when they're playin' fur the Ashes!'

✦   ✦   ✦

It was Alistair Burns' funeral. As he had been a keen Nationalist all his days, a piper met the cortege at Craigton crematorium, and accompanied the coffin and undertakers into the chapel.

Afterwards, Happy Harry was discussing the day's events with Jammy. 'That wis a helluva racket they pipes made in the crematorium the day.'

'It certainly wis,' replied Jammy. 'At first ah couldnae make up ma mind if it wis a funeral for Burns, or if they were piping in the haggis fur him!'

✦   ✦   ✦

After the funeral the gravediggers were busy filling in the grave.
It was hard work on a hot day.

'You boys take a good drink?' asked Jammy.

'Oh, aye, Mister Stewart,' they replied in unison, eyes
lighting up.

'Well, let the fellow in that grave be a lesson tae you!'

+   +   +

Jammy was told by Laughing-Boy that girlfriend, Flora
MacDonald, had competition, as the widow of a local minister
had her eye on him. 'Ye know, she's been merrit three times noo,'
Laughing-Boy told him. 'The first wan worked in a bank, the
second wan was an actor and then she married a meenister. Noo
she fancies you, an undertaker, fur a wee change,' he laughed,
giving Jammy a nudge.

'Och,' observed Jammy. 'it chust sounds like it's wan fur the
money, two fur the show, three tae get ready and four tae go!'

+   +   +

'Mister Stewart,' enquired the widow. 'wid it be okay if ah pit some stuff in the coffin alang wi' ma man?'

'Well, yes, madom,' replied Jammy cautiously. 'depending, of course, on what it is, as it's a cremation.'

'It's jist auld fitba programmes. He always bought wan when he went tae the match, an' noo they're fair cluttering up the hoose!'

✝   ✝   ✝

Jammy contacted the crematorium staff. 'See the funeral fur auld Jeanie MacDougall this afternoon,' he said. 'Well, the family have requested an Elvis number as she wis a big fan o' his. See whit ye can dae, wull ye?'

Later that afternoon, as the family of auld Jeanie entered the crematorium, they were regaled with Elvis singing, '*Return to sender, address unknown*'.

✝   ✝   ✝

Jammy was in the pub, as usual having a cordial blether with Tottie. 'As you're an undertaker,' observed Tottie, ' ah've got to tell you. Ah've made up ma mind no' tae attend any more funerals'

'Och, that wouldna be polite, nutatall,' observed Jammy indignantly. 'Efter aw, if you don't go to your friends' funerals, they won't come tae yours.'

✝   ✝   ✝

7

'Dead Jammy' and the traffic warden

'That's another ticket on Lazarus' windscreen, Jammy.'

'Another yin, Rip! That's the second this week!' exclaimed Jammy, steam coming out of his ears. 'Has that traffic warden, Sadie whitshername oot there, nothing better tae do in life than put bits o' paper on hearses? Ah'm chust gonnae huv a word in yon's lug, indeedy ah am.'

So saying, and without putting on his jacket, he lifted his burning cigar and strode out of the front entrance of Stewarts. Immediately, he saw the culprit across the road, busily writing out another ticket before sticking it under the windscreen wiper of a car.

'Here, you! Ah want a word!' shouted Jammy, storming across the road. 'Whit's the big idea pittin' a parking ticket oan oor hearse again? It's an absolute desecration o' the departed, that's whit it is, indeedy so. The profession o' undertaking is surely exempt fae this sort o' thing?'

'Mister Stewart, how many times have we had this conversation?' replied an unflustered Sadie. 'Ah've telt ye afore, an' ah'll tell ye again, if a motor vehicle is in direct contravention of the law and beyond the stipulated time shown, then, regardless of its business, ah will carry oot ma duty, which is whit ah'm paid fur. So there!'

'Ah think you would book yer faither,' yelled Jammy in frustration.

'Ah've already booked him, twice!'

'Heavens above have ye nae humanity? Chust a wee bit o' charity,' begged Jammy. Then, seeing she was stony-faced, he decided to change tack. 'Listen, Sadie, let's be reasonable. You're like me. You have a very responsible position in this community. But let's be realistic. Ye wouldnae stick a ticket on ma hearse if it wis the funeral o' wan o' yer ain family, would you now?'

'Naw, because ah wid be aff duty an' at the funeral,' replied the cool Sadie. 'But if ah saw wan o' ma colleagues booking ye that day, then ah widnae object. They'd be quite right.'

'But, Sadie,' pleaded Jammy. 'You're being awfu' unfair on every family in this district. Ah need tae recover ma overheads, so ah chust add on yer fines tae ma funeral costs.'

'It's nane o' ma business whit ye dae. Ah'm here as a representative o' authority.' And shoving out her chest, she turned, and was about to move on when the owner of the car she had just booked rushed up. 'Ah'm awfa sorry,' gasped the agitated lady motorist, 'but ah had a long wait at the doctor's surgery. But that's me back noo.'

'It doesnae matter if that's you back,' snapped the officious Sadie. 'Wance ma paperwork is completed, that's it final.' Then

off she went prancing along the street, meticulously checking her wee book for other victims.

'Wid that no' sicken ye?' observed the woman turning to Jammy. 'That yin's nae feelings. Ah know whit ah wid like tae dae tae yon.'

'Aye, so dae ah, madom, but hanging's been abolished,' replied Jammy, and he went back indoors.

'Ah'm gonnae swing fur that Sadie,' he informed GFT, as he marched back into his office.

'Ah don't think Jammy is o'er fond o' that traffic warden,' observed Rip to GFT with a smile.

'Ye cannae blame him. Imagine putting tickets on a hearse. Ah widnae dae that.'

'Listen, GFT, if you were a traffic warden, you would book the polis!'

The following day Lazarus broke down again, this time it was right in front of the parlour. With the 'Faunty' refusing to start and another funeral due shortly, Jammy urgently phoned the RAC.

The RAC patrolman had tended to Lazarus a number of times before. 'Ah've told you, Mister Stewart. There's something funny aboot this motor. Maist o' the time ah cannae find anything wrang wi' it. If ye ask me there's a wee gremlin in the works somewhere. Dae ye think that a hearse could be haunted?'

'Naw, the only thing that haunts me aroon here is that Sadie! She must've booked this hearse half-a-dozen times in the last couple o' months.'

'Don't talk tae me aboot that wan, Mister Stewart. She's booked ma RAC van umpteen times. Ah think there must be a competition amongst they wardens tae see who can raise the maist revenue. An' that Sadie's jist got tae be the winner!'

However, the following Monday a new traffic warden appeared. This one proved to be much more reasonable. Lazarus could be left outside for as long as Jammy liked, despite standing on yellow lines. Jammy thought he would show his appreciation, so he popped out to chat to see the new warden and give him a cigar.

'How are you enjoying this beat?' asked smiling Jammy.

'Aye, it's fine,' replied the man. Clearly he was a helpful, friendly individual. 'The problem is it's only temporary until Sadie comes back tae work.'

'Oh, is she on holiday, or something?' enquired the no longer smiling undertaker.

'Naw, naw. She's in the Western Infirmary fur tests. She wis apparently feeling awfu' dizzy. They think it's maybe her blood pressure.'

'Aye, well, she certainly pits mine up.' observed Jammy. 'Maybe ah should send her some flowers. That might just do the trick. Maybe make her a bit more reasonable when she comes back.'

The flowers, from Flora MacDonald's flower boutique, were sent to Sadie's ward. The accompanying card read. 'We hope you get well. Eventually yours, Signed James Stewart,'

But two weeks later Sadie was back on her beat, and within an hour had booked Lazarus. When Jammy found out he immediately hunted her down. 'Listen, Sadie, when you were away a nice wee man replaced you and he didnae put any parking fines on oor hearse. How come now that you're back we're booked again? His interpretation of the rules is obviously different from yours'!'

'Well, Mister Stewart,' said Sadie. 'Ah can tell you that he's wrang and ah'm right. Ye've jist been lucky, that's aw. But noo ah'm back ah'll be keeping ma eye oot fur that hearse o' yours, an' if it is incorrectly parked ah will take the appropriate action. It'll take mair than a bunch o' flooers tae change me. So, there!'

Jammy was boiling. He stormed back into the parlour muttering threats about writing to the Lord Provost and the Prime Minister. But of course he didn't.

A month and two parking fines later, there was a commotion outside the parlour. GFT went out to investigate and reported back that Sadie had apparently fainted. Jammy and Rip Van Winkle went outside. There was a small crowd around Sadie, who was lying on the pavement. 'Don't worry,' instructed Jammy. 'We'll look after her.' And with that he and Rip lifted her into the parlour. 'Right,' said Jammy. 'Into the preparation room wi' her.'

'But she's no' deid, Jammy!' remonstarated Rip.

'Ah know, but help me get her intae a coffin, quick!'

As Sadie was being lowered into the coffin, her eyes fluttered and opened. Sadie looked directly up at Jammy, just as he put the lid on top.

'I'm alive! I'm alive! I'm back! I'm back!' came her faint but urgent voice from within.

'Sorry,' Jammy said dryly. 'But wance the paperwork's complete that's it final!'

However, after five minutes of listening to her scream he relented. Sadie was helped out of the coffin and given a cup of tea, which her shaking hands just about managed to hold. Jammy then had her taken home in one of the limos.

And from that day on, Jammy never received another parking ticket!

+　　　+　　　+

Dead Funnies

'Hey Jammy,' said Tottie. 'Dae ye think that folks in Scotland tend tae shove death under the carpet?'

'Och, nutatall,' came the reply. 'Sure there wid be a horrendous lump.'

'Anyway, Jammy,' observed Tottie. 'It's no' a problem fur me. Ah'm gonnae live forever, or die in the attempt.'

+　　　+　　　+

Jammy was going over the details of a forthcoming funeral with the eldest son of the family.

'I believe yer father owned a bakery?' he said.

'That's right, Mister Stewart.'

'And have you, kind sur, thought of the wording for the Notice of Death?'

'Well, ah have, Mister Stewart,' replied the son. 'You see, ma faither wis a man of few words, so he always said he just wanted, 'Mister Reid, fae Parkheid, is deid, so there's nae breid'.'

'Well, we can insert that if you really wish,' replied Jammy doubtfully. 'And have you a request for music at the crematorium?'

'Aye, he had a favourite hymn. 'Bread of Heaven'.'

+　　　+　　　+

'He was a campanologist doon at the local parish church every Sunday morning,' explained Laughing-Boy, talking about one of their 'customers'. 'Aw the woman fair fancied him. Apparently they thought he looked like Cary Grant.'

'Och, well,' observed Jammy, 'he's certainly a dead ringer noo.'

+   +   +

'Hoo did it happen?' asked Jammy.

'He went doon tae the shops fur ma *Record*, and just drapped deid,' said the widow.

'So, whit did ye dae?'

'Ah jist listened tae the radio instead.'

+   +   +

'How's business, Jammy?' asked Tottie the barman.

'Terrible. Ah huvnae buried a living soul since Tuesday!'

+ + +

The old lady came in to see Jammy about a pre-arranged funeral plan. A few years back she had been in about the same thing, but had decided not to sign up.

Jammy took her through the cost of the various elements of a funeral. 'Mister Stewart,' she said, 'yer prices have fair gone up since the last time'.

'Och, madom, it's chust the high cost of living increases.'

+ + +

The wee man stood at the graveside of his recently departed wife. She had been a notorious nagger and henpecker, someone who was generally disliked by everyone because of her unpleasant disposition.

Just as the minister finished the final committal, there was a terrific clap of thunder directly overhead. The widower turned to Jammy and observed with a wee smile, 'Sounds like she's arrived, Mister Stewart.'

+ + +

'Did that cough mixture the doctor gave yer auld uncle straighten him oot?' asked Tottie.

'Och, aye,' replied Jammy. 'Ah'm burying him himsel' the morrow.'

+ + +

As Jammy was making his way along a path in Sighthill cemetery, he met a woman and her dog.

'Moarnin',' said the lady politely.

'Naw, madom,' Jammy replied, 'ah'm jist going tae see if a grave has been dug yet.'

+ + +

Jammy had been talking to a lady who had come to see him about a pre-paid funeral arrangement plan for herself. However, after going over the details, she seemed reluctant to sign the form.

'Och, ah'll tell ye whit, madom,' said Jammy. 'Jist take yer time tae make up yer mind. You should sleep on it, and if you wake up in the mornin', jist let me know.'

She signed.

✦　　✦　　✦

'Whit's the death rate in Glasgow, Jammy?' asked Tottie.

'Och, 'tis the same as everywhere else in Scotland, Tottie. This government only allows wan death per person.'

✦　　✦　　✦

'How would you like tae die, Jammy?' asked Tottie.

'At ninety-five fae terminal bunions, wi' a malt whisky drip right intae ma veins. And of course, wi' ma boots oan,' came the laughing reply.

'Oh, jist like the cowboys?' replied an open-eyed Tottie,

'Och, nuttatall. If ah didnae huv ma boots oan, then, when ah kicked the bucket ah might injure ma toes!'

✦　　✦　　✦

The eldest son was talking to Jammy about his father's funeral arrangements. 'Dae we get money aff if he disnae wear a shroud?'

'Wid ye like him buried in a suit, then?' countered Jammy.

'Naw, naw. He wis a nudist. Ma mither wants him buried in the scuddy.'

✦　　✦　　✦

'What kind o' Glaswegians go tae heaven dae ye think, Jammy?' asked Tottie.

'Deid wans.'

✦　　✦　　✦

'You know, Mister Stewart,' said the widow tearfully. 'he wis aye saying, 'Ah never died a winter yet'.'

'Well, he wis right, madom, indeedy he was. This is the Glasgow Fair ... July!'

+   +   +

One day, just before a burial, Jammy noticed a card attached to a wreath. He quickly snatched it off and phoned the florists. 'Och, ma wee flower,' he said to Flora, the owner of the shop and his sometimes girlfriend. 'Ye've made a wee bo-bo this time, indeedy ye have. We're jist aboot tae set aff fur the cemetery and wan o' yer wreaths has the wrong card on it. It should say,'In loving memory'. Instead you've got, 'Congratulations on your new abode'!'

+   +   +

'Had a hard day, Jammy?' asked Tottie.

'Och, cannae grumble,' came the reply. 'Though at wan funeral this morning, a mourner drapped deid at the graveside. Ah can tell ye it fair cast a right gloom over the whole proceedings.'

+   +   +

The woman had come in to see Jammy to make arrangements for her own pre-paid funeral.

'Ah want cremated and ma ashes scattered in Arran,' she informed him.

'And why Arran, madom?' asked Jammy.

'Well, ah've heard it's a nice place, an' ah've never been there afore!'

✚   ✚   ✚

'You must sing a lot o' hymns every week, going tae that crematorium so much,' observed Tottie one evening.

'Yer right, Tottie,' replied Jammy. 'the wan that gets me is *Abide Wi' Me*. Ah don't want tae abide wi' deid folks fur years an' years!'

✚   ✚   ✚

The two sons came to see Jammy about their father's funeral.

'Could ye no' jist stick him in a plastic bag and burn him?' they asked.

'Och, ye cannae dae that, no indeedy,' replied Jammy, aghast. 'Tell ye whit. Ah think ah hud chust better have a word wi yer mither on the phone.'

After talking to their mother, Jammy spoke again to the two brothers. 'Yer mither has asked me tae tell ye something very personal. Apparently she and yer father never married.'

'Ye mean we're ...'

'Indeedy so,' commented Jammy, 'and right stingy wans at that!'

✚   ✚   ✚

'An' whit, madom, wis yer man wearing when he drapped deid?' Jammy asked the widow.

'A dirty big smile. He'd jist come in fae the pub.'

✚   ✚   ✚

8

'Dead Jammy' and the funeral tea

Monday morning, drizzle, and Lazarus had broken down, again. The problem was they were on their way to a funeral at Riddrie Park Cemetery, where they were to meet up with the principal mourners at the graveside. All efforts to resuscitate the stricken vehicle had failed, and the hearse sat embarrassingly by the side of the road, silent as the grave.

Jammy looked in despair at his pocket watch. He closed his eyes and prayed to the God he had heard mentioned many times a day, and promised the great spiritual leader all sorts of things if he would just come to his aid and provide a miracle, just a wee one, to get his hearse working. Jammy's eyes opened, and he realised the great spiritual high-heid-yin was out to mock him, as Laughing-Boy again tried the ignition key and Lazarus refused to wheeze, never mind start. And just when he thought things couldn't get any worse, along came the new Co-op hearse, sleek and polished. Inside the C-op staff grinned openly at his plight.

'By chove, this isnae your day, Jammy,' muttered the undertaker to himself. It certainly wasn't, for at that very moment there was a cloudburst. The rain didn't take time. Then, as Jammy huddled miserably under his umbrella the 'man upstairs' relented. Joe the joiner drove up in his van and stopped. 'Anything ah can dae tae help, Mister Stewart?' he enquired.

Jammy's first thought was, 'Aye, how aboot paying me the twenty pounds ye still owe fur yer faither's funeral?' But instead he wailed, 'Joe, chust the man! Ma hearse has developed a wee condition, nothing much really. Any chance o' helpin' us oot, ma good frien'?'

Joe's eye glinted. 'If ah dae, will it be worth the twenty quid ah still owe ye?'

'Och, man, chust you help me oot the day and we'll be saying nae mair aboot that wee drap o' money,' replied a desperate Jammy.

'Fine, whit can ah dae, then?' smiled Joe.

'Ah need tae get auld Mrs McGhee's coffin tae Riddre Park Cemetery, right noo. We're a wee bitty late. Dae ye think ye could accommodate it in the back o' yer van, plus masel' and Laughing-Boy here?'

'Maybe,' replied Joe. 'But wan o' ye will need tae get in the back wi' the coffin as there's only a wee seat here beside masel'.'

'That'll be no problem. Ah'll chust go in the back,' said Jammy.

The coffin was deposited into the back of Joe's van, much to the astonishment of passing motorists. Jammy then crawled in beside it only to find that the back of Joe's van was covered in wood shavings. 'By jove!' he thought as Joe's van started off. 'It's been some morning.' With the morning's problems behind him Jammy relaxed. Then, as the van rumbled along, he became pleasantly sleepy.

Suddenly, the back doors of the van burst open and a cold blast of air and splashes of rain hit Jammy's face. He woke with a start and realised he had an audience. Heavens, the principal mourners! They had arrived! Quickly Jammy scrambled from the van. Laughing-Boy dusted the shavings from the back of his coat. Hands grabbed the coffin, quickly moving it over to rest on the cross-planks above the grave.

Jammy drew out his list of those people allocated cords. As

he passed the first card to the principal mourner, the man whispered, 'There had better be a good explanation fur delivering ma maw here in a van.'

'Dinnae you worry, Mister McGhee, ah know it doesnae look good, but yer mither would be pleased wi' the way we dealt wi oor wee emergency.'

'Ma mither wouldna have been pleased at all, Mister Stewart!' retorted the man. 'She enjoyed ill-health. Ah'll have you know she wis on and aff her death bed fur the last fifteen years. Wan minute she wis at death's door. The next she wis oan a plane tae Benidorm. She wis looking forward tae her funeral an' gettin' delivered here tae the cemetery in a gleaming hearse. An' noo you've spoiled the hale thing fur her. However,' said the son, fixing Jammy with a meaningful look, 'ah'm confident that ah'll no' be gettin' any bills fae ye fur this fiasco. The papers jist love wee stories like this, don't they?'

A despondent Jammy made a determined effort to ensure there were no further hiccups at Mrs McGee's funeral. He fussed around around at the graveside, and the rest of the funeral went off as planned, apart from one of the party slipping on the wet grass. 'Definitely no' ma day!' thought Jammy.

Jammy returned in a taxi, squeezed in with the mourners. The funeral party were then dropped off at a small hostelry, the *Tartan Bunnet*, for tea, sausage rolls and sandwiches, allowing Jammy to thankfully return to the funeral parlour. He quickly arranged for the local garage to try to weave their magic on Lazarus.

He had just put the receiver down, when the phone rang again. Normally he would have let GFT deal with it, but some instinct made him snatch it up.

'Em, Mister Stewart, this is Sandy, the manager o' the *Tartan Bunnet*. A voice said. 'We've goat a wee problem, but ah don't really want tae call the polis. Ye gie us quite a bit o' business, efter aw, but it's your funeral party. Ye see, wance this lot finished their tea, they got stuck in at the whisky, an' noo there's a terrible argument going on; a right kerfuffle. Ah think it's aboot who gets their maw's stuff. Can ye come o'er right noo an' sort it oot?'

'Ah'm on ma way, Sandy,' replied Jammy. Whit a day this is

proving tae be, he thought. Auld Mrs MacGhee seems tae have put a curse on her funeral. Everything seems tae be going wrang.'

As Jammy approached the *Tartan Bunnet* he could hear raised voices. 'This isnae going tae be easy,' he thought. 'Sounds as though they're aw well fu'.'

Walking into the room where the funeral tea was being held, he rapped his umbrella loudly on the door. It proved a good strategy, as the room fell silent.

'Heavens above, Mister McGhee, kind sur!' said Jammy, addressing himself to the deceased's son. 'Whit is the problem? The manager's threatening tae call the polis!'

'Aye, well let him!' growled a red-faced McGhee. 'They can charge ma brother wi' robbery while they're here!'

'Robbery? Why, whit's been stolen,' asked Jammy.

'Ma maw's kitchen table. Hector here says ma mither left it tae him, but she told me, wan o' the times she wis oan her deathbed, that the kitchen table wis mine!'

'A kitchen table?' laughed Jammy incredulously. 'Ah've had families arguing aboot money in a will, but never o'er a kitchen table.'

Hector folded his arms and looked sullen. 'It wis ma mother's.' he said. 'It would be nice tae huv some memory o' her. She promised it tae me.'

'How much is it worth?' asked an exasperated Jammy.

'Ye'd be lucky tae get a fiver fur it at the Barras,' chipped in one of the other mourners. 'Ah've seen it. Widnae gie it hoose room, so ah widnae.'

Jammy was fed up, frustrated. He decided to take the bull by the horns. 'Right, tell ye whit,' he said. 'Ah'll gie ye twenty quid fur it. That's a tenner each. How's that?'

After a moment's consideration, the elder of the two brothers said, 'That's a real bargain, Mister Stewart, especially as we're getting the funeral fur free, courtesy o' Joe the Joiner's van, remember?' And he winked wickedly at Jammy.

'Right,' said Jammy, ignoring the dig and taking out his wallet. 'Everybuddy here can witness this. Ten pounds each tae baith o ye, on wan condition, mind! Ye aw go hame, right noo. Ah've other funeral parties coming in here an' ah don't want ony problems fae the management.'

'Fair enough,' smiled the younger brother. 'Maw would be fair pleased at the bargain o' a funeral she has had. And don't you worry, we'll make sure her auld table is delivered roon tae yer parlour.'

Sure enough, the following day, auld granny McGee's table was delivered to Stewarts, or rather it was dumped at the door. It had clearly seen better days. 'Pit it in the store room alang wi the coffins,' Jammy told Rip.

A few hours later there was a timid knock at Jammy's office door.

'Come in,' called Jammy.

Looking up he saw Fred, their part-time French polisher.

'Can ah see you a wee minute, Mister Stewart?' he enquired.

'Certainly, Fred. Nice tae see you. You know you dae a great job fur us, so ah hope your no' going tae tell us your leaving or something?'

'Naw, naw, Mister Stewart,' said Fred. 'Nothing like that. Ah wis jist wondering if you would like tae sell me that table in the storeroom. Maybe ye didnae ken but ah collect antiques, and that table's is one of the best I've seen.'

'Och, right,' said Jammy, now all ears. Looking at Fred he laid it on thick. 'Well, ah don't know, Fred, he said. 'It's an auld family heirloom. So, it is really awfa special. Worth a lot o' money that table,' he added in a knowing manner.

'Well, fur a William the Fourth mahogany table like that ah could maybe manage, say five hundred pounds, Mister Stewart. In cash, of course.'

'Five hundred pounds!' choked Jammy. Then quickly recovering himself, added, 'Aye, well you've been a very good servant tae Stewarts, so ah could chust maybe let you have it fur that.'

'Thanks Mister Stewart! It's no' often a get a chance at such a lovely bit o' furniture.'

In the *Pigs and Whistles* that night, Tottie asked how Jammy's day had gone. 'Aye, pretty fair, Tottie. In fact ah'll have another dram.' Then shocked Tottie by adding, 'And have one for yoursel'.'

As Tottie turned to get the drinks, Jammy thought, 'Ah would have charged the MacGhees four hundred and fifty pounds for their mother's funeral. Add Joe the Joiner's twenty, then the thirty pounds to have Lazarus fixed and the twenty fur the table. Aye, chust maybe the 'high-heid-yin' up there did answer ma prayers efter aw, indeedy so!'

And he smiled.

+ + +

Dead Funnies

'Have you lived in Glasgow all your life?' Jammy asked the widow.

'No' yet,' came the reply.

+ + +

The man was clearly dying. He had the look of 'wet clay' about him. 'Wan thing, Mister Stewart,' he added, when the details of his funeral had been agreed. 'ah want ye tae tell everybody ah died o' Aids.'

'Aids? But, surely that's no' yer problem.'

'Ah know. But ma wife is a good bit younger than me. Ah don't want her sleeping wi' other men.'

+ + +

'If you're no' keen on dying, Tottie,' explained Jammy to the barman, 'then ye should change yer surname tae wan that starts wi' 'z'?'

'Wull that keep me alive?'

'Naw, but ye can see fur yersel' in the *Evening Times* that folks in Glesca tend tae die in alphabetical order!'

+ + +

'Ah'm sorry yer dear wife has died,' said Jammy to the widower.'Ma condolences tae you and yer family, kind sur.'

'Thanks very much, Mister Stewart,' replied the man. 'It happened awfi' sudden like. This morning when ah felt her, she wis stone cauld all over. Ah cannae understand it, fur she was hot in bed last night.'

+ + +

'Hey, Jammy,' said Tottie. 'A've goat a terrible pain in ma chest the day. Dae ye think ah'm gonnae die.'

'Och, dinny be daft,' replied Jammy. 'That's the last thing you'll dae!'

+ + +

'It's been awfy quiet in the bar fur the past hour, Tottie. Is there a big match oan the night?' asked Jammy.

'No' that ah know o',' replied Tottie. Then he suddenly added, 'Don't tell me, Jammy, ye've parked Lazarus ootside again?'

'Och, no! Ah huv that. Ah better away hame. An' ah've a coffin in the back tae!'

+ + +

'How did yer mother die?' Jammy asked the eldest son.

'Well, she was always a bit hot tempered, you see,' came the reply. 'She was in the local chippy; liked fish suppers, ye ken. She was arguing with Lou that he hadn't gie'd her any chips, when she suddenly drapped deid.'

'Well, she's certainly had her chips noo!' Jammy quipped.

+   +   +

The man came in to pay the bill for his wife's funeral.

'And how is efferything with you?' asked Jammy sympathetically.

'You know, Mister Stewart,' said the widower. 'I'm so miserable without her. It's almost like having her back.'

+   +   +

Jammy was going through various aspects of the husband's funeral with the widow. 'Dae ah get a discount, Mister Stewart?' she asked. 'Efter aw, he only had wan leg. The ither yin wis widden.'

'Sorry, madom, but the costs are just the same, indeedy so. Though some folks might say that's a matter o' a pin yin.'

+   +   +

'Never a day's illness in her life, Mister Stewart,' moaned the bereaved husband. 'In fact she wis never constipated until after she died.'

'Huh? Och, right then,' replied a somewhat confused Jammy.

+   +   +

'And how would you like your ashes disposed of, madom?' Jammy asked the lady, who was organising her own funeral with Stewarts.

'Jist sprinkle them at the door o' that bar at the corner o' the Trongate.'

'At a pub? Jings, madom, if I may say so, that's unusual. Indeedy it is. Can ah ask you why?'

'It's so ma husband will pay his respects tae me every night fur a change.'

+   +   +

As Jammy was getting out of his hearse outside his funeral parlour, a Glasgow worthy approached him. 'Excuse me, Jimmy, but ur youse an undertaker?'

'Yes, indeedy ah am,' replied Jammy, somewhat warily. 'Can ah be of any assistance?'

'Ye might,' replied the man. 'Ye see, ma auld uncle is jist aboot deid.'

'Ah'm sorry to hear that,' replied Jammy courteously. 'So how can ah help?'

'Well, he doesnae huv only life insurance,' explained the man, 'an' ah wis jist wonderin' if ye did 'homers'?'

+   +   +

'He wis a good man, so ma Peter wis,' said the widow to Jammy. 'Though he wisnae ony good wi' the money side o' business. He took oot a life insurance policy but it didnae dae him ony good. He died anyway.'

+   +   +

'And ah want ma man tae have a fish-supper coffin, Mister Stewart,' said the widow. 'Ma next door neighbour had her man in wan o' them an' ah thought it awfa nice.'

'Ah think yer maybe a wee bit mixed up there, madom, indeedy ah do,' said Jammy, stifling a smile. 'Ah think you're talking aboot the wan that has a motif o' the Last Supper on it!'

+   +   +

At the crematorium Jammy had a quiet word with the grieving widow.

'How old wis yer husband, ma dear?' he asked, his voice full of concern.

'Ninety-nine. Jist a year older than masel',' she whispered.

'Och,' observed Jammy, his unfortunate sense of humour coming to the fore, 'on a cauld winter's day like the day, it's hardly worth yer while gaeing awa' hame.'

+   +   +

'Whit wis yer family history up in Skye, Jammy?' asked Tottie.

'Och, ma family always followed the medical profession.'

'Were they doctors?'

'Nutatall! Sure they were undertakers chust like masel'.'

+   +   +

LAST REQUEST: BURIAL INSTRUCTIONS

And does it have to be Ibrox?

'So, madom,' asked Jammy, after the arrangements for the funeral were agreed, 'is there anything else?'

'Jist wan thing, Mister Stewart,' she said. 'A couple o' hours afore he died ma man swallowed a gold filling, and we were sort o' waitin' for it to come oot again, if you know whit ah mean. Ah don't suppose there is anyway of retrieving it noo?'

'Och, I'm afraid not, indeedy no,' replied Jammy.

That evening in the pub, Jammy related the story of the widow wanting the gold filling back. 'Ah tell ye, Tottie. The only way tae get that tooth back wid be if he woke up, found himsell deid in his coffin, an' shit himsel'!'

✛   ✛   ✛

Laughing-Boy and Jammy went to pick up a body at the Western Infirmary morgue.

'We've come for Mister MacAllister,' explained Jammy to the morgue attendant.

'Sorry,' said the man, 'he's still in ward six. Ah'm afraid he wisnae quite as deid as we first thought!'

85

✛   ✛   ✛

'Dae ye think there's such a thing as reincarnation, Mister Stewart?' asked the widow.

'Naw, madom, ah doubt it. Indeedy ah do.'

'But whit if there wis?'

'Och, in that case ah wid make oot a will leaving everything tae masel'!'

✛   ✛   ✛

9
'Dead Jammy' and the body in the cemetery

'How do you keep so healthy, Jammy? Ye never seem tae be either up nor doon.'

'Och, it's simple, Laughing-Boy, indeedy so,' replied the funeral director, clearly in a good mood. 'Every morning ah take a brisk walk to the cooker. Then ah make masel' porridge. Ma faither did the same, and he lived till he was ninety.'

'Well, if you're that fit, you won't have life insurance, then?'

'Och, man, ah do indeedy. Everybuddy should have some.

But you've got to watch the kind o' policy ye get. As the Good Book says, 'The big print giveth but the small print taketh away'.'

'So you read the Good Book?'

'Indeedy. Ah've got life insurance fae the Prudential fur this life, and fire insurance oot the Good Book fur the next. So ah'm chust laughin'.'

'Phone call for you, Jammy,' interrupted GFT's voice from the foyer. 'Says it's urgent, and they only want to speak tae you.'

Jammy lifted the phone. 'Mister Stewart here, can I be of assistance to you?'

'There's a body lying in Rutherglen cemetery,' gasped a woman's excited voice.

'There are thoosands o' bodies lying in Rutherglen cemetery,' countered Jammy.

'Aye, but this one's noo lying under a bush.'

'Oh, right then. Jist leave it tae Stewarts the undertakers. Thanks fur lettin' us know.' Hanging up he exclaimed, 'Quick, Laughing-boy, start up Lazarus. You and me's fur Rutherglen cemetery. We might chust get ourselves a bit o' business.'

But they found the cemetery to be quiet, very few visitors about, and certainly no sign of any body. 'Did the person on the phone say whereabouts this body was supposed to be?' asked Laughing-Boy.

'Naw, she didnae say. Chust that it wis lying under a bush. We'll chust have to keep looking. Wance we find it, we'll need tae phone the polis.'

'That phone call might o' been a hoax, Jammy. It's no' as if we huvnae had them afore.'

'Aye, true, but this lady sounded authentic.'

It was on their second circuit of the cemetery that Laughing-Boy saw something moving between two gravestones. 'Ah think there's somebody over there,' he said, pointing ahead. He put his foot down and Lazarus put on a spurt. Then they saw the body. The trouble was it was stark naked, moving, and obviously very much alive.

'Och, it's chust some nutter knocking aboot the cemetery in the scuddy,' pronounced a disappointed Jammy. 'We'd better just away back tae the parlour and call the polis.'

The words were hardly out of his mouth when 'the body' ran towards them, hands strategically placed. 'Stop!' came a desperate voice. 'Ah need yer help!'

'Stop Lazarus, wid ye?' Jammy demanded. 'But lock the doors. This could be the nutter to end all nutters.'

A naked young man stood before them, cold, trembling, and covered in mud.

'Please help,' he pleaded. 'Ah'm getting married today an' ah need to get home tae get ready. Ma fiancée will kill me if ah let her doon.' He was desperate, and obviously sane. Jammy lowered a window.

'Whit happened tae ye, man? Yer naked as the day ye were born, an' muddy tae.'

'It wis ma stag night last night, an' ah got a bit fu',' explaimed the young man. 'Aw ah can remember is ma pals getting me oot the pub, then ah've a vague memory o' coming alang the road tae the cemetery. They must've put me intae a grave that wis dug ready for a funeral. When ah wakened up, ah can tell ye ah sobered up fast. Ah had a terrible job climbing oot. Then ah terrified two auld biddies who were walking along a path nearby.'

'Indeedy, no wonder,' said Jammy. 'It wis probably one one of the auld wifies who phoned the parlour. An' whit did the ladies say when they saw you?'

'They just screamed, hysterically. Probably hadn't seen a naked man in years.'

'So then what did you do,' asked Jammy.

'Ah jist lay doon behind some bushes. Then ah saw your hearse. Whit's the time noo, mister,' he asked.

'It's two o'clock,' replied Jammy.

'Fur heaven's sake, ah'm getting' married at three! Wid ye dae us a big favour an' get me hame so ah can get dressed fur ma wedding?'

'Ok.' agreed Jammy. 'We cannae leave ye in this state. Jist lie doon in the back. We'll pit a cover o'er ye.'

When they got to the fellow's home, he said, 'Ye've been awfy good, Mister Stewart. But could ye hold on fur five minutes till ah throw on ma gear? Then ye could maybe gie me a lift tae the church. It's just roon the corner fae your parlour. Ah'd be eternally grateful.'

'Aye, okay. On ye go. We'll wait,' said Jammy. Turning to Laughing-Boy he remarked. 'Not only didn't we get any business oot o' this wee adventure, noo we find ourselves acting as a wedding taxi. If we dae this again we'll need tae tie white ribbon on tae Lazarus' bonnet.'

Before long the young man, resplendent in a kilt, came rushing back to the hearse.

'Ah've got two minutes tae get tae the church,' Mister Stewart. 'They'll aw be wondering whit's the matter. Apart fae ma rotten mates, that is.'

Laughing-Boy whizzed Lazarus to the church at a speed previously unknown for the hearse. Outside the church, Jammy quickly opened the back of the hearse, and again let the young man out.

'Thanks for the lift,' said the groom. 'Ye've baith been great. But ah must say it wis awfy unfomfortable lying in the back o' yer hearse.'

'Well, let me tell you something, son, indeedy ah will' replied Jammy. 'You're the first person ever tae climb oot the back o' this hearse and complain!'

✦   ✦   ✦

Dead Funnies

Jammy was going over the funeral arrangements with the widower.

'Noo,' said Jammy. 'we can arrange for your funeral party to have tea and sandwiches at the local restaurant, or haute cuisine at the *Tartan Bunnet* Hotel.'

'Och, a cauld menu will dae fine, rather than the hot wan.'

✦   ✦   ✦

'Have ye ever envied ony o' yer deid 'customers'?' asked Tottie.

'Och, indeedy,' replied Jammy. 'In fact quite a few times. Efter aw, when ye think o' it, wance yer deid yer made fur life!'

✦   ✦   ✦

'Ah've goat tae tell ye, Mister Stewart,' said the widow. 'He wisnae the best o' husbands. Och, well, at least there's wan good thing aboot this life. It's only temporary.'

✦   ✦   ✦

'You'll never believe this, Jammy,' exclaimed an agitated GFT. 'Ah've jist had a wuman on the phone. Her fourth husband has died and she wants us to do the cremation. Four husbands! Ah ask ye. Ah cannae get wan, and she spends aw her time burning them!'

+   +   +

'Did your husband die following an operation?' Jammy asked the widow.

'Naw, naw, Mister Stewart,' replied the widow. 'In fact the only operation he ever had in his life was on his private part, tae make it circus sized.'

+   +   +

'He always said he wanted a wee verse put in his death notice, Mister Stewart,' said the widow. 'It's jist a silly wee poem really. Could you perhaps stick it in the paper?'

'Let me see it, madom, and I'll tell ye,' replied Jammy. The undertaker read the poem before pronouncing it suitable. It read:

'Here's tae purridge when yer hungry,
Whisky when yer dry.
Aw the lassies in the world,
An' Heaven when ye die.'

+   +   +

I kept on telling him you can still have all the ciggies and sex and booze same as ever, but please not the deep-fried Mars bars. Not now you're 97.

'It's a funny thing,' observed the widow. 'Ma husband wis born on a Saturday. We first met at a dance on a Saturday. We were married on a Saturday. His mother died on a Saturday, and his faither died on a Saturday.'

'And when did your husband pass over?' asked Jammy.

'Last Tuesday.'

+   +   +

'Hey, Jammy,' exclaimed Tottie, as he saw the undertaker coming into the bar. 'You're the very man tae answer this question.'

'Well, ye know ah always do ma best tae give ye advice.'

'Right then, Jammy. Here's the question. If yer scared half tae death twice in the wan day, is that you deid?'

+   +   +

'Ah've come tae see you oan a most serious matter,' said the Glasgow cooncillor to Jammy. 'In fact, in your business you could say it was a grave concern. Ye see, ah've had complaints fae ma constituents.'

'Complaints? Aboot Stewarts the Undertakers? Surely no, kind sir,' replied Jammy, immediately concerned.

'Well, mostly aboot wan thing, really,' continued the cooncillor. 'Apparently that hearse o' yours keeps breaking doon during funerals. It's distressing tae ma constituents. So ah'm here tae demand ye buy a new wan.'

'Replace Lazarus?' exclaimed Jammy. 'Ah've goat tae tell ye, Cooncillor, Stewarts the Undertakers is a community business. We look efter oor customers, indeedy we do. We like tae keep oor prices doon. So, if ye want us tae buy a new hearse, Glesca Corporation wull need tae guarantee us a minimum number o' deaths every year!'

+   +   +

'Well, he always worried aboot his health,' said the widow to Jammy. 'He always felt bad when he felt good for fear he'd feel worse when he felt better. So noo he's maybe better aff feeling deid.'

'Indeedy, so,' replied a somewhat confused Jammy.

✦　　✦　　✦

'Jammy,' said Tottie in the bar one night. 'Ah've another question fur you.'

'Listen, Tottie,' replied Jammy, 'if there is such a thing as reincarnation you'll come back as Magnus Magnusson.'

'Aye, well, ah've started so ah'll finish. You know how you sell folks a pre-payment plan fur their funerals? Well, have you personally put anything away fur a rainy day, Jammy?'

'Och, indeedy aye,' came the smiling reply. 'A pair o' wellies an' an umbrella!'

✦　　✦　　✦

The two Glasgow men sat across the desk from Jammy. 'Willie and masel' have come tae see you regarding two funerals. Ye see, Willie lives up the stair fae me an' his mother-in-law who stays wi' him has just died. Ma Uncle Kenny in the next close has just died tae. So, we wiz wondering, dae Stewarts the Undertakers have a 'buy wan, get wan free scheme'?'

✦　　✦　　✦

'Are ye goin' tae the golf club's Christmas 'doo' this year, Jammy?' asked Tottie.

'Indeedy not, ah'm afraid, Tottie,' moaned Jammy. 'Ye see, maist o' ma friends are noo deid.'

'Och, Jammy,' protested Tottie. 'Ye could surely dig somebuddy up?'

✦　　✦　　✦

'He wis a lovely artist, ye know, Mister Stewart,' said the widow. 'Did awfu' nice portraits an' landscapes. Probably sittin right noo in Heaven paintin' a picture o' something.'

Jammy just couldn't resist. 'Aye, still life,' he quipped.

+ + +

'Hey Jammy!' asked the ever-inquisitive Tottie. 'Dae ye really think there's ony way tae stop gettin' old?'

'Aye. Next time yer driving doon the road, try having a wee sleep at the wheel.'

+ + +

Tottie was once more in contemplative mood. 'Hey Jammy, ah wis jist thinking. Why do clerics at a funeral no' jist use the same words they use at a wedding? 'For better or for worse' could surely mean the person is either goin' tae heaven or tae hell.'

'Naw, naw, Tottie man, they couldna use these words,' Jammy replied. 'When the minister or priest says, 'For better or for worse' at a wedding, whit he really means is that the groom couldnae dae better an' the bride couldnae dae worse!'

+ + +

EARTH
To EAR -

'Ah'm afraid wan o' yer regulars died the day, Tottie. Aye, auld Peter McAlpine,' said Jammy.

'Peter McAlpine! No! Away tae hell,' exclaimed the shocked Tottie.

'Aye, probably,' said Jammy.

+   +   +

'Ye see, Mister Stewart,' sobbed the widow. 'Ma husband could be a bit cantankerous. He didnae like oor doctor, Doctor McDougal.'

'Och, ah see,' muttered Jammy.

'Aye,' said the widow. 'Ah think he jist died tae humiliate the poor man!'

+   +   +

'Ah hope ah don't start greetin' in the crematorium, Mister Stewart,' said the widow, tearfully.

'Listen, madom, that would be a very natural thing to do, indeedy it would. So don't you worry aboot it. If you feel like a wee greet, chust you do it,' replied Jammy.

'Thanks for your kindness, but you see, Mister Stewart, ah wis really thinking o' a wee daft saying ma man kept coming away wi'.'

'And what would the wee saying be, madom?'

'Well, he always said, 'Laugh and the world laughs with you, cry and you huv tae blow yer ain nose!''

+   +   +

'Are ye feart o' death, Jammy?' asked Laughing-Boy.

'Naw, nuttatall,' replied the undertaker. 'Sure only the good die young. Anyway, Heaven wull be chust like Glesca.'

'Dae ye really think there wull be Glaswegians in Heaven?'

'Listen,' said Jammy. 'Saint Peter wid be feart no' tae let them in!'

+   +   +

Jammy and Rip Van Winkle went to the Royal Infirmary mortuary to collect a patient who had died. While there, Jammy and Rip went into the cafeteria for a cup of tea, and got into conversation with a trainee nurse.

During the chat Jammy let slip the name of the ex-patient they were collecting. 'Oh, aye, Mister Miller,' said the nurse. 'He wis an awfu' nice wee man. Do you know, his wife told me that he had never been fatally ill before, until he woke up deid this morning!'

+   +   +

'Ah felt it wis time tae come an' make ma arrangements,' said the old gentleman to Jammy.

'Very wise, kind sur,' replied Jammy. 'It's good tae pit yer mind at rest. And how is your health?'

'Oh, ma health is no' bad,' replied the man. 'Naw, naw, that's no' the reason ah'm here. It's because ah wis always brought up by ma parents to respect ma elders, and noo it's getting' harder and harder tae find ony.'

+   +   +

Final thought

The secret of longevity is deep breathing. All you've got to do is keep it up for years and years. Try each day to beat your own previous record for the number of consecutive days you've stayed alive!

And remember, as Jammy Stewart, he himsel', might have said. 'It's no' the cough that carries you off, it's the coffin they carry you off in!'

✦   ✦   ✦